Palgrave Studies in Cyberpsychology

Series Editor
Jens Binder, Nottingham Trent University, Nottingham, UK

Palgrave Studies in Cyberpsychology aims to foster and to chart the scope of research driven by a psychological understanding of the effects of the 'new technology' that is shaping our world after the digital revolution. The series takes an inclusive approach and considers all aspects of human behaviours and experiential states in relation to digital technologies, to the Internet, and to virtual environments. As such, Cyberpsychology reaches out to several neighbouring disciplines, from Human-Computer Interaction to Media and Communication Studies. A core question underpinning the series concerns the actual psychological novelty of new technology. To what extent do we need to expand conventional theories and models to account for cyberpsychological phenomena? At which points is the ubiquitous digitisation of our everyday lives shifting the focus of research questions and research needs? Where do we see implications for our psychological functioning that are likely to outlast shortlived fashions in technology use?

More information about this series at
https://link.springer.com/bookseries/14636

Andy Phippen · Louisa Street

Online Resilience and Wellbeing in Young People

Representing the Youth Voice

Andy Phippen
Computing & Informatics
Bournemouth University
Poole, UK

Louisa Street
Falmouth, UK

Palgrave Studies in Cyberpsychology
ISBN 978-3-030-88633-2   ISBN 978-3-030-88634-9   (eBook)
https://doi.org/10.1007/978-3-030-88634-9

This Palgrave Macmillan imprint is published by the registered company Springer Nature
Switzerland AG
The registered company address is: Gewerbestrasse 11, 6330 Cham, Switzerland

ACKNOWLEDGEMENTS

This work is based upon a five-year project, and we are indebted to the work on Ben Bolton at Cornwall Council and Dr. Sarah Canavan-King at King Psychology in the project's early stages, speaking with young people and professionals and laying the foundations that ultimately led to research findings that underpin the Online Resilience Toolkit and its subsequent professional development opportunities.

CONTENTS

CHAPTER 1

Introduction

Abstract Many professionals working with safeguarding responsibilities faced a two-pronged challenge of a lack of effective resources and training to support them, and personal experiences bleeding into the professional judgements. The Headstart Kernow project undertook a youth-focussed approach to understanding their use of digital technology and their needs of support from professionals in navigating these digital worlds.

Keywords Online safety · Digital resilience · Digital value bias · Critical thinking

Teacher:	They play these violent video games, then they're violent in school.
Andy:	No, there isn't much evidence of that.
Teacher:	Well I've seen it.
Andy:	There really isn't—this is a causation policy makers and the media have been trying to show for over 40 years and there is no evidence of it existing.
Teacher:	Well, that's what I reckon. They shouldn't be allowed to play them.

© The Author(s), under exclusive license to Springer Nature
Switzerland AG 2022
A. Phippen and L. Street, *Online Resilience and Wellbeing in Young People*, Palgrave Studies in Cyberpsychology,
https://doi.org/10.1007/978-3-030-88634-9_1

The above is the paraphrasing of an exchange that took place during a training session in the project about which this book is written. The training was to broadly explore the issues arising from many discussions with young people related to "online safety"—the frequently discussed and, it seems, poorly understood term generally associated with the need to keep children "safe" online.

The training, which is discussed in more detail in Chapters 5 and 6, aimed both to explore attendees' knowledge of the "online world" and to also give them confidence in supporting young people who might be disclosing problems they are facing related to online harms. During this training, there is a focus upon moving away from the technology, focussing on behaviours and bringing in fundamental safeguarding practices such as disclosure and support. One of the key messages delivered is bringing objectivity to safeguarding judgements. In general, attendees were very much in agreement about this approach. However, as we will discuss in later chapters, while it might seem like a simple concept to deliver in a training setting, it seems far more difficult to bring to practice.

This book considers the state of online safeguarding through the lens of a five-year youth mental health project, established in 2016, called Headstart Kernow.[1] However, this is not an exploration of the Headstart Kernow project per se, more an exploration of online safeguarding and tensions between policy, adultist views and the youth voice. We make use of the extensive research in the project as vehicle for this exploration. We will, throughout this book, present a youth voice that, in contrast to the views of many professionals and policy makers, does not ask for prevention or prohibition from online harms, but understanding and support when things go wrong. It poses a fundamental question:

> How can professionals best respond to young people who disclose they are victims of online harm?

There is a supplementary, but equally important question, particularly given the discussions around online safeguarding policy in Chapter 2:

> How can we provide young people with a safe, supportive environment so that they are confident that they can disclose that they are a victim of online harm, and know they will get support?

[1] https://www.headstartkernow.org.uk/. Accessed August 2021.

We will explore in depth our discussions with young people of the duration of this project in subsequent chapters and what arose from these conversations—a key issue that repeatedly emerged was what we might refer to as *digital value bias,* where professionals will bring views about the safeguarding in a particular scenario, or a general view, that is underpinned not by professional training and objective reasoning, but opinion informed without authoritative source and conjecture. The quotation at the start of this chapter is a good illustration of this. The teacher was clearly uncomfortable with "age inappropriate" games and talked about the violent and sexual nature of some of the games the student played. It was their view that this was not acceptable, and young people under aged should not be playing them. This is a view that is entirely acceptable and one with which we do not particularly take issue. It is their opinion and that is to be expected. However, claiming a causation without evidence is something with which we would disagree. Yet this is something we have observed repeatedly through our project work, and also in our wider working practices.

One young person (aged 17) we spoke to during the project stated clearly:

> I don't listen to adults when it comes to this sort of thing.

When asked why they felt this, they said firstly adults tend not to understand online issues and, because they do not have similar online experiences to young people, they tend to overreact to situations and instead of providing support, make things worse.

Another was a discussion early in the project with a headteacher at a school in Cornwall demonstrated that perhaps this young person was correct to feel this way. They were asked what their incident response process is for dealing with a "sexting incident"—a typical situation being where a young person has self-produced an intimate image of themselves and then sent it to some who has non-consensually shared it further. Again paraphrasing, the response from the head was:

> We usually get the DSL to give them the hairdryer treatment first, so they don't do it again, then we see what we can do to help

This in an issue that we will develop in Chapter 2 and return to in Chapter 6, because sexting does present professionals with a challenge given the criminal nature of the act of a young person self-producing an intimate image and the need to, in the view of many professionals, prevent young people from doing this.

Which brings us to the other recurrent theme, that of the *online white knight*—adults who see it as their role to eliminate harm, or the risk of harm, with young people's interactions online. They wish to keep them safe online, and therefore, they must eliminate the risk of harm. They need to *prevent* harm. As we will discuss during this book, this is an attitude we have encountered with many professionals. Their intention is worthy and admirable. It is also, for reasons we will explore later, a pipe dream.

THE HEADSTART KERNOW PROJECT

The project was a partnership programme to develop resilience and mental wellbeing in young people in Cornwall that was led by Cornwall Council and funded by the Big Lottery. The project's stated aim was to adopt a "trauma-informed" approach to children's mental health support in the county that was[2]:

- *focused on young people aged 10–16 as evidence clearly demonstrates that half of diagnosed lifetime mental ill-health cases begin before the age of 14, and 75% before the age of 18;*
- *co-produced with young people who inform and influence it and are key stakeholders;*
- *universal, and about prevention with targeted support;*
- *a 'Test and Learn' programme;*
- *striving to achieve system change;*
- *doing things differently—we embrace new and innovative ways of thinking and working and people are at the forefront of what we do.*

From the early stages of the project, a youth voice was considered a fundamental aspect. The project made it clear that the starting point should be listening to young people and helping them consider the resilience and

[2] https://www.cornwall.gov.uk/health-and-social-care/mental-health/help-me-feel-mentally-stronger/. Accessed August 2021.

mental health challenges they face. A young people's council was established to inform the project from proposal to strategy to delivery. From those early stages of the project, a number of clear messages from young people were communicated:

- *We want to be able to understand our own thoughts and emotions and can talk openly when we need help.*
- *People around us need to know the signs and know what to do when we are struggling.*
- *Help must be reliable and consistent; we will know who we can trust to help us to help ourselves.*
- *We are helped to cope with the pressures of life, including online.*
- *We learn and share what we have learnt.*

And what was clear from these early discussions with young people, online pressures are real and present in their lives. It was equally clear, therefore, that online had to be part of the project.

The Headstart Kernow project itself was underpinned by the seminal work of Bronfenbrenner and his ecological framework of child development (Bronfenbrenner, 1979).

In Bronfenbrenner's framework, he described different systems they operate around a child that has direct or indirect influence upon them. Simply expressed, these are:

- **Microsystem**—The child's immediate environment, such as home, family and close friends.
- **Exosystem**—People and places that have an indirect impact on the child's life, such as their wider community, formal and informal education settings, social care, healthcare settings, etc.
- **Macrosystem**—Government policies and cultural values, including laws, social values and economic drivers.
- **Chronosystem**—The influence of change and constancy in a child's environment, acknowledging that the child's environment, and influences, will change over time.
- **Mesosystem**—Different parts of the child's immediate environment interacting together.

This ecosystem of interconnections facilitates the development of the child and highlights the different, and equally important, roles players in the system have. A critical aspect to note about this ecosystem is that it clearly shows that there is no one independent entity that ensures positive development of the child at the exclusion of others. It is an ecosystem of cooperative individuals and organisations and the interactions between them that results in healthy development. Perhaps most importantly in his model, and perhaps lacking when we consider online safeguarding, was the importance of mesosystems—the interactions between the different players in child development.

A Youth Voice and a Refocussing of the Discourse

While there were many activities within the Headstart Kernow project, we will focus on the work around what was referred to as the "Digital Resilience workpackage". This was established to develop a youth-led strategy around how online technology impacts upon young people's wellbeing and to develop strategies to better inform professionals about how they might be supported. We wanted to do something different from the typical "online safety" approach, which is to develop resources, whether these be videos, lesson plans or documents that "help" young people think about their behaviour online and conduct it in a safer manner.

Within this book, we will use the findings of the workpackage as the vehicle to explore challenges in child online safeguarding and why/how we need to bring more of a youth voice to the discourse.

Alongside our experiences within the Headstart Kernow project, we also draw upon previous experiences as an academic and a youth worker with, collectively, over thirty years' experience speaking to young people about these sorts of issues. As such, the discussions are driven from an ethnographic, as well as empirical, perspective and we will incorporate a lot of personal narrative. Given the participatory nature of both our roles in the Headstart Kernow project (one as the lead for the digital resilience workpackage and the other as the facilitator of the digital research strategy), and our wider work with young people, it would be disingenuous to present this analysis without a reflexive perspective.

This is not, like much research into child online safeguarding, an objective survey-based method. While these are entirely appropriate for this area, and works such as the EU Kids Online project (Livingstone et al.,

2011) have been instrumental in informing policy, this is not our chosen approach. As we will discuss in early chapters, we started from a position of not knowing the relationship between emotional wellbeing and online behaviours affecting young people. Therefore, it seemed that the most appropriate approach was to ask young people directly, build our understanding, and then consider potential interventions. In adopting an immersive approach alongside aims to strongly represent the youth voice, we hoped to move conversations away from prevention to support and empowerment, for both young people themselves and also stakeholders in their safeguarding.

The chapters in the book are broken down to firstly define the project aims against the context of online safeguarding policy and then explore how we came to the outcomes we achieved. Particular to this exploration was a tool that we developed what become known as the Headstart Kernow Online Resilience Tool (Headstart Kernow, n.d.), a resource developed for those working in the children's workforce to assess behaviours disclosed by young people, and the associated risk, and included in this book as an appendix. While the tool is a core outcome from the project, it is not the concluding part of this book—the development of the tool is a fundamental part of the exploration of youth voice in online safeguarding, and it is a means to an end rather than an endpoint of itself. What will become clear through this exploration is that while the tool, and subsequent training developed within the project, provided us with a tangible output to attempt to start addressing culture change in online safeguarding, it is, as with any resource, not going to change culture of itself.

In presenting this research, findings and evaluation of impacts, the book is broken down into five main chapters, along with final conclusions.

In Chapter 2, we introduce the overall aims of the Headstart Kernow project, the challenges presented with aligning online behaviours with the chosen approach and the broader fit with the online safeguarding context. While this has been introduced above, we will explore in more detail in this chapter.

Chapter 3 develops these findings against a wider, personal, exploration of prior experiences working with young people and the challenges faced by professionals in talking about online issues with them. This chapter develops themes from discussed above and in Chapter 2, but introduces more explicitly a differentiation between safety and resilience explaining why, even though it is not without its challenges, taking a resilience-based perspective, informed by a professional understanding of risk and harm reduction, is more inclusive than preventative discourses.

In Chapter 4, we present the foundational work, which was formed of semi-structured discussions with a range of young people to gain better understanding of their views, concerns and wishes around online safeguarding. These discussions helped us better understand the tension between preventative agendas and how these were at odds with young people and, in some cases, became barriers between them and those with safeguarding responsibilities.

Chapter 5 discusses the development of the Online Resilience Tool in more detail but always keeping a broader view around why the tool was developed how it was, and how young people were included in its development. Again, we illustrate that the inclusion of youth voice in the development of these sort of resources continues to challenge value biases and assumed harms.

Chapter 6 explores the impact of the tool and how it has been used to change attitudes towards online safeguarding through the use of resilience discourse and providing professionals with a practical tool to challenge their prejudices. It also reflects at length about experiences in training and working with professionals, and how we can slowly move towards a victim centric and less knee-jerk response to online safeguarding disclosures. However, it also discusses how difficult some of these deeply held beliefs are to challenge.

Finally, in Chapter 7, we bring the discussion to a close with further reflections on how we can move conversations around online safeguarding forward by adopting an approach that is underpinned by youth voice and supports stakeholders in safeguarding. It also reflects upon changes that have occurred in the wider online safeguarding world since the development of the tool—namely COVID lockdowns and the Everyone's Invited website of disclosures of youth sexual harassment and abuse—to consider how the lessons learned in the Headstart Kernow project might reach a broader audience.

References

Bronfenbrenner, U. (1979). *The ecology of human development: Experiments by nature and design*. Harvard University Press (ISBN 0-674-22457-4).

Headstart Kernow. (n.d.). *Headstart online resilience tool*. https://www.headstartkernow.org.uk/digital-resilience/. Accessed August 2021.

Livingstone, S., Haddon, L., Görzig, A., & Ólafsson, K. (2011). EU kids online. *Final Project Report*.

CHAPTER 2

The Online Safeguarding Landscape

Abstract The "online safety" policy area is beset with preventative views and an overreliance and expectation for technology to prevent harm. Current online safety policy has a history of prevention that can be seen to have its roots in controlling access to pornography. Legislation that has arisen in the last ten years has similarly adopted a preventative approach, yet young people consistently tell us that "online safety" is either boring or ineffective. Even the term "online safety" is doomed to fail—we cannot ever hope to prevent harm online; however, we can equip young people with the knowledge to understand, and mitigate, risk when online.

Keywords Online safety · Digital resilience · Algorithms · Critical thinking · Stakeholder perspectives

This chapter places the Headstart digital resilience workpackage in the wider context of online safeguarding. This allows us to then explore findings from conversations with young people against the current "leading edge" of policy thinking. Drawing extensively from UK legislation and policy, this chapter presents an analysis of the online harms agenda—a safeguarding approach that endeavours to keep children and young people safe online by preventing them from being exposed to adultist

© The Author(s), under exclusive license to Springer Nature
Switzerland AG 2022
A. Phippen and L. Street, *Online Resilience and Wellbeing in Young
People*, Palgrave Studies in Cyberpsychology,
https://doi.org/10.1007/978-3-030-88634-9_2

definitions of harm, with an expectation that platform providers can pro-actively tackle any potential harmful activity via algorithmic means. The critical analysis of these approaches, drawing upon previous work in the field, demonstrates the lack of youth voice, and the complete disregard for their rights, in this policy direction.

What Do You Mean by Safe Anyway?

In one of our early discussions, a young man challenged the notion of safety online, which brought the reality home to us:

> What do you mean by safe anyway?

His view, articulated very clearly, was that we cannot ensure someone can go online without being presented with some risks—he spoke about gaming with people one doesn't know and the risk they might be abusive, group chats where someone could say something mean and seeing upsetting content when browsing for other things.

In this young man's view, you could not prevent these things from happening when going online, but you can help young people understand that these things might happen, and help them if they are upset when they do. This was not a view that said we should stop trying to talk about online risk, because of course this is important. However, he was of the view that you cannot prevent online harm and pretending you can does not help young people.

One of the fundamental challenges we will explore within this book, drawing extensively on our discussions with both young people and professionals, is that we start from a position of prevention with the term "online safety". We have used this a number of times already within this book, and the use of quotes is deliberate. A lot of online safeguarding discourse draws analogies from road safety—we have frequently heard comments about how "we teach them how to cross the road safely, and we should do the same for being online". However, this is applying an adultist perspective on safety and attempted to transfer it onto a domain where it is inappropriate.

Let us consider road safety, there are few threats but the main one is serious and can cause a young person serious harm—if they are struck by a car while crossing the road. Therefore, we can put simple rules in place to mitigate this risk. We can tell children to look both ways before crossing, make sure they have clear view up and down the road, listen out for traffic and make use of the tool available within the road environment (such as pedestrian crossing systems) to further mitigate that risk. The focus is entirely upon the prevention of an accident between child and motor vehicle.

If we compare this with the online world—firstly what are the threats? There are many and range from exposure to upsetting content, abuse by peers, unsolicited sexual contact by predators, non-consensual sharing of indecent images, being hacked and having identity data from being shared and so on. And, in contrast to the road environment, which is well controlled, with established standards (e.g. cars travel on roads, pedestrians travel on pavements) and a stable environment (it would be unusual to wake and discover we had decided that cars should now travel on the opposite side of the road to the day before), new online risks emerge as the digital infrastructure evolves and develops. Unlike the "atomic" world of roads, digital environments have few boundaries other than the ever expanding capacity of networks upon which all online services operate, and the imaginations of the developers who put services and platforms in place for billions of citizens to use, which poses the question:

- *What rules can we put in place to make sure a child is **safe** online?*

Preventative Approaches to Online Safety

If we take a broadly accepted definition of safety—that something is free from risk or harm—we are sadly chasing a utopian goal that will never be achieved in the online world. There is a way to ensure a child is safe online—we take their digital devices away from them and make sure they have no means to be online. Therefore, they will not be exposed to the risk that exists there. However, we will undoubtedly also be preventing them from the many positive experiences that can be delivered online. So, we reject disconnection as a viable safety route and instead bring other preventative measures to the online safety conundrum. For example, two popular preventative views are:

- *We wish to stop young people seeing upsetting content. Lets filter content to stop the young people seeing it.*

- *We wish to ensure a young person isn't taking and sending intimate images. They should be told its illegal and they should not do it.*

However, if we begin to unpick these issues, we get ourselves into a further tangle. If we wish to prevent access to "harmful" content through some sort of filtering, we need to understand what we mean by this. The Reporting Harmful Content service,[1] provided by the UK Safer Internet Centre to support young people who have been exposed to harmful content, details harmful content in a number of categories:

- Threats
- Impersonation
- Bullying and harassment
- Self-harm or suicide content
- Online abuse
- Violent content
- Unwanted sexual advances
- Pornography
- Terrorist content
- Child sexual abuse imagery

It is not the intention of this book to now consider each of these forms of content, the capability of algorithms to detect it (this is done in far more detail in Phippen & Brennan, 2019) or further approaches that could be adopted to prevent access. However, we will briefly explore a perennial favourite in the online safeguarding policy world—preventing access to pornographic imagery.

Again, a noble cause—while young people we speak to are generally of the view that they are comfortable with (or at least resilient to) pornographic content, they also invariably have the view that access is something we should prevent for younger children.

This is typical for most, regardless of age—they believe they are fine, but those younger would not be. This is a manifestation of the *third person effort* phenomenon (Davison, 1983), a belief as a subject that they are fine, but others may be affected or harmed more significantly. While the origins of the theory lie in mass media communication, it has

---

[1] https://reportharmfulcontent.com/. Accessed August 2021.

also been applied to subject matter as diverse as hip-hop lyrics (McLeod et al., 1997), violence on television (Hoffner et al., 2001) and online pornography (Lee & Tamborini, 2005).

In our wider experiences in discussions with young people (e.g. see Phippen, 2016), there are on occasions indications of the negative impact of pornography access on young people. We have met young people with performance and size anxiety which we would hypothesise is related to exposure to pornography. Equally, a lot of young people we have spoken to have stated that they believe it gives unrealistic expectations around sexual activity. While causation is difficult to prove (e.g. see Horvath et al., 2013), there are few that would argue for unrestricted access to pornography for young people.

However, prevention is a challenge, as can be seen from efforts for well over ten years to address this problem. The "solution" over this time has been filtering technologies, which make use of software that can identify pornographic materials and prevent access either through matching website addresses or identifying sexual keywords on a website. Once the filtering algorithm has identified a website is providing pornography content, it will block it. While this is a well-established practice in schools (and a statutory expectation as defined in Keeping Children Safe in Education (Department for Education, 2021), the UK Government document that defined safeguarding expectations on schools in England and Wales), the social/home environment presents some challenge. Overblocking is a fundamental challenge with filtering systems—they will block websites that are not providing access to pornography but instead are using similar sexual keywords—for example sites that might support relationships and sex education. While this is an accepted part of internet access at school (where systems can be modified to "bypass" filters to access educational resources), overblocking in the home environment can be more frustrating, particularly when parents will neither have the time or knowledge to manage their filters at a fine level of detail.

Digital technology is very good at clearly defined rule-based functionality in easily contained system boundaries. Or, to put it another way, data processing, analysis and pattern matching of data. Computers are very good at taking data and analysing it based upon rules defined within the system (e.g. identify words that *might* relate to sexual content). However, they are far less good at interpretation and inference or, to use a current popular term for these sort of systems, intelligence.

By way of an illustrative, albeit trivial, example, let us take the word "cock". This is a term that might be related to a sexual context—it could to male genitalia. Equally, it might refer to an avian animal. If we consider this from the perspective of a filtering system, that might be tasked with ensuring an end user cannot access websites of a sexual nature, that system might be provided with a list of keywords that could indicate sexual content. It would be expected that "cock" would be one of these terms. The filtering system would be very good at pattern matching this string of characters to any mentioned within any given website and would, as a consequence, decide the site contained pornography content and block it. We use the term "decide" advisedly—the algorithm has no capability to make a decision in the way a human might, it is merely responding to rules coded into it by a developer. As such, the algorithm is far less good at determining the actual context of the website—it *might* be about sexual activity; however, it might also be about animal husbandry.

Even with this simple example, we can see how it might struggle to prevent access to all sexual content or, equally, result in *false positives*— blocking innocuous[2] sites that are not "inappropriate" for children to see. Another simple and popular example of this comes from the overblocking of the Northern English town of Scunthorpe (Wikipedia, n.d.).

The flaws in filtering systems, still viewed as the best approach to preventing young people from accessing pornography, have attracted the attention of the United Nations, who have concerns that while being successful at preventing access to some pornography (but providing no barrier to pornography shared on social media or peer-to-peer communication) they might impact significant upon human rights. The "Report of the Special Rapporteur on the promotion and protection of the right to freedom of opinion and expression" in 2018 (United Nations Human Rights Council, 2018) stated that:

> States and intergovernmental organizations should refrain from establishing laws or arrangements that would require the "proactive" monitoring or filtering of content, which is both inconsistent with the right to privacy and likely to amount to pre-publication censorship.

---

[2] We will use the term "innocuous" sites to describe those who have been incorrectly blocked based upon the requirements of the filter (e.g. pornography, gambling, drugs and alcohol) and not "legal", because access to pornography is legal in the UK.

We have, in other work (Phippen, 2016), raised concerns about the *safe-guarding dystopia*, where an overreliance on technical solutions and an obsession with prevention leads to a safeguarding environment that fails to support young people and instead impacts negatively on their human rights and freedoms.

This brief review looked at prevention of access to one type of fairly unambiguous "harmful" content—pornography. The challenges for algorithmic intervention increase further when considering even more subjective and ambiguous content, such as violent or terrorist content. We do not plan to elaborate upon further technical interventions here, but we hope the point we are making is clear—preventing access to all of these types of harmful content is perhaps not the most progressive approach to supporting children and young people in their online experiences and it is certainly not a complete or particularly successful approach.

We take the second example, which considers the sending of a self-produced intimate image by a young person using their mobile device. We have, in Chapter 1, explored a response to this type of incident with one school. And while the response is not one we would support, we are sympathetic, because with this scenario, there are further challenges.

By the letter of the law (specifically, section 1 of the Protection of Children Act 1978 [UK Government, 1978]), any young person taking an intimate image of themselves, and sending it to someone else, is breaking the law. Of course, this legislation was never intended to address this scenario—it was developed to protect young people from exploitation in the production of "pornography" (more correctly child abuse imagery—for further detail, see Phippen & Brennan, 2020). However, there is no provision in the legislation to say "if the subject is also the taker of the image and sender of the image, and is a minor, this is not a crime", and it has never been modernised, so the law still stands. We know, from many conversations with young people (explored in more detail throughout this book), that this is the key educational message delivered to them—"don't send nudes, it's illegal". If a minor is subsequently subject to abuse as a result of the image being non-consensually shared further, there is a serious and legitimate safeguarding concern. It would seem, in our experiences, that it is the intention of professionals that the mere mention of the legality of the practice is a preventative tool to eliminate this potential harm and keep young people safe.

We would, in an ideal world, wish for the young person to disclose this non-consensual sharing and be supported by safeguarding professionals.

Indeed, if the victim of non-consensual sharing was an adult, this is exactly what they could do, with protection in law (section 33 of the Criminal Justice and Courts Act 2015 [UK Government, 2015]). However, the fact the young person is breaking the law by taking the image in the first place (under the 1978 legislation) and they have been told this through their school life, are they likely to disclose, or are the more likely to suffer in silence?

THE YOUTH VOICE

Young people have a different perspective. When conducting research projects in 2009 and 2021 around teen sexting (Phippen, 2016), one question we posed for our survey respondents was "what can adults do to help if someone is upset by a sexting incident". The three most popular responses were:

- Listen
- Don't judge
- Understand

While the initial work in 2009 was survey based and did not provide us with the opportunity to explore these responses in depth, qualitative discussions in 2012 did. What was clear was that the wish for young people was they wanted to be able to disclose harm and get help, not a telling off or judgemental statements like "You shouldn't have taken those images in the first place". Such attitudes exist in other youth-focussed studies around sexting, such as Emily Setty's highly young person centric work (Setty, 2020). And we still see these wishes with the conversations we draw from the Headstart Kernow work, presented in Chapters 4 and 5.

ONLINE SAFETY POLICY

Online safety has, arguably, existed as a safeguarding requirement in schools for fifteen years, but did not become part of any statutory framework until more approximately nine years ago. The two major changes to this online safety landscape have been the inclusion of online safety as part of the OFSTED, the schools regulator of England, inspection framework in 2012 (OFSTED, 2013) and its inclusion in the Department for Education's (DfE) Keeping Children Safe in Education statutory guidance since 2015 (UK Government, 2021). If we consider the latest requirements regarding online safety in school settings from the Department for Education, we can see there are requirements around training:

14. All staff should receive appropriate safeguarding and child protection training (including online safety) at induction. The training should be regularly updated. In addition, all staff should receive safeguarding and child protection (including online safety) updates (for example, via email, e-bulletins and staff meetings), as required, and at least annually, to provide them with relevant skills and knowledge to safeguard children effectively.

89. Governing bodies and proprietors should ensure an appropriate senior member of staff, from the school or college leadership team, is appointed to the role of designated safeguarding lead. The designated safeguarding lead should take lead responsibility for safeguarding and child protection (including online safety).

117. Governing bodies and proprietors should ensure that, as part of the requirement for staff to undergo regular updated safeguarding training, including online safety (paragraph 114) and the requirement to ensure children are taught about safeguarding, including online safety (paragraph 119), that safeguarding training for staff, including online safety training, is integrated, aligned and considered as part of the whole school or college safeguarding approach and wider staff training and curriculum planning.

Management of risk:

128. Whilst considering their responsibility to safeguard and promote the welfare of children and provide them with a safe environment in which to learn, governing bodies and proprietors should be doing all that they reasonably can to limit children's exposure to the above risks from the school's or college's IT system. As part of this process, governing bodies and proprietors should ensure their school or college has appropriate filters and monitoring systems in place. Governing bodies and proprietors should consider the age range of their children, the number of children, how often they access the IT system and the proportionality of costs vs risks.

129. The appropriateness of any filters and monitoring systems are a matter for individual schools and colleges and will be informed in part, by the risk assessment required by the Prevent Duty. The UK Safer Internet Centre has published guidance as to what "appropriate" filtering and monitoring might look like

And curriculum:

> 119. Governing bodies and proprietors should ensure that children are taught about safeguarding, including online safety, and recognise that a one size fits all approach may not be appropriate for all children, and a more personalised or contextualised approach for more vulnerable children, victims of abuse and some SEND children might be needed

However, there is nothing in the document that defines *what* online safety training or curriculum should look like (non-statutory guidance from the DfE on teaching online safety was released in 2019 (Department of Education, 2019). The management of risk centres mainly on ensuring appropriate technology is in place to make sure inappropriate content cannot be viewed, and online activity is monitored with appropriate alerts are in place should abuse occur. Furthermore, while we know that Keeping Children Safe in Education makes it clear that online safety should form part of whole school safeguarding training, we know from other work (SWGfL, 2021) that 40% of schools (in a sample of 12,000 schools) have no training in place.

Further clarification of the view of online safety (and safeguarding) from the policy perspective could be seen in 2018's Online Harms White Paper from the Home Office and Department of Culture, Media and Sport (UK Government, 2018), which defined a large list of potential harms that can occur online, and proposed a legislative framework and expectation on service providers to mitigate harm. In essence, online safety has become a preventative and prohibitive method of ensuring young people are free from harm through a mix of control, filtering and poorly defined education. Yet with poorly defined expectations, we cannot be surprised that young people's views and experiences with online safety can vary immensely and professionals view online harms as something that need to be stopped, rather than mitigated or managed.

Nevertheless, the preventative approach continues and arguably becomes strong. At the time of writing, the UK Government has published their draft Online Safety Bill 2021 (UK Government, 2021) and it is portrayed in the media as the UK Government's crowning glory in making "Britain the safest place to go online in the world". While we will explore the Bill in a little more depth in this book, it is not intended that there will be a detailed examination of all 145 pages of the draft bill.

However, it does illustrate once more national policy level thinking on what online safety looks like. The prevailing view is that the heart of online safety is a "duty of care" for online service providers. It is down to them, and the bill is clear, to make sure citizens in the UK are not exposed to illegal material and what is also referred to as "legal but harmful". It is clear that companies that cannot demonstrate duty of care will be found liable for abuse that happens on their platforms, however complex this negligence might become.

What is particularly unclear is whether the duty of care in the bill being defined as related to a form of negligence as defined in civil law? If so, how might the company be able to demonstrate due diligence or protect itself from vexatious or unsubstantiated claims of harm? It would seem, however, that the government is indeed introducing failure to protect from online harm as a form of negligence for which one might make civil claim. While we anticipate much contested legal debate on liability, given what is actually possible through the tools available to platforms (such as algorithmic detection and reporting tools), it is clear the expectation by government is that harms can be stopped.

Changing the Perspective

If we now return to the conversation that started this book should we really be surprised that this teacher has this view. Given the nature of online safety is one that has been beset with preventative messages, and the "leading edge" of policy thinking is further efforts at prevention, why should a professional not think that prevention is the best approach? Of course they will bring their own lived experiences to their views they develop, especially given the dearth of training available to professionals. Without effective training, or training that perhaps reinforces preventative messages, the gaps in knowledge will be filled with conjecture and existing biases.

We will explore this in more depth in later chapters, but one of our key observations from our work across the project is that professionals will bring their social and family experiences into their professional judgements. Given that we use digital technology in our own social and personal lives, we can bring this into our professional expectations. This is, of course, quite inappropriate for a professional safeguarding judgement, particularly given that most knowledge developed around the use of digital technology is done so in an informal and ad hoc manner, but it is something have consistently observed through this work. To continue with road analogies, we would not expect one's capability to drive a motor vehicle be a good foundation knowledge to diagnose a serious mechanical issue with a school minibus. Or, to put it another way, our social knowledge is no substitute for professional development.

In conclusion, in this chapter, we have explored the initial goals of the Headstart Kernow project against the broader domain of online safety policy. While the goals of the project were to be inclusive and strongly represent the youth voice, online safeguarding policy, and the views of professionals who work in the domain, is strongly preventative.

While there are good intentions with these views, they immediately create a tension between those wishing to protect and those who might need protecting. This tension is further tightened with a dearth of professional knowledge around online safety being in filled with opinion and conjecture, such that there is a belief that online technology has a negative impact upon young people's wellbeing, without having the empirical evidence to underpin this view. In the following chapter, we develop the source of this tension further, with a reflective exploration by one of the authors of this book (Louisa) in over ten years of experience as a youth worker.

References

Davison, W. P. (1983). The third-person effect in communication. *Public Opinion Quarterly, 47*(1), 1–15.

Department for Education. (2019). *Teaching online safety in schools.* https://assets.publishing.service.gov.uk/government/uploads/system/uploads/attachment_data/file/811796/Teaching_online_safety_in_school.pdf. Accessed August 2021.

Department for Education. (2021). *Keeping children safe in education 2021—Statutory guidance for schools and colleges.* https://assets.publishing.service.gov.uk/government/uploads/system/uploads/attachment_data/file/999348/Keeping_children_safe_in_education_2021.pdf. Accessed July 2021.

Hoffner, C., Plotkin, R. S., Buchanan, M., Anderson, J. D., Kamigaki, S. K., Hubbs, L. A., Kowalczyk, L., Silberg, K., & Pastorek, A. (2001). The third-person effect in perceptions of the influence of television violence. *Journal of Communication, 51*(2), 283–299.

Horvath, M. A., Alys, L., Massey, K., Pina, A., Scally, M., & Adler, J. R. (2013). *Basically... porn is everywhere: A rapid evidence assessment on the effects that access and exposure to pornography has on children and young people.* https://eprints.mdx.ac.uk/10692/1/Basica. Accessed August 2021.

Lee, B., & Tamborini, R. (2005). Third-person effect and internet pornography: The influence of collectivism and Internet self-efficacy. *Journal of Communication, 55*(2), 292–310.

McLeod, D. M., Eveland, W. P., & Nathanson, A. I. (1997). Support for censorship of violent and misogynic rap lyrics: An analysis of the third-person effect. *Communication Research, 24*(2), 153–174.

OFSTED. (2013). *Inspecting eSafety.* https://www.eani.org.uk/sites/default/files/2018-10/OFSTED%20-%20Inspecting%20e-safety.pdf. Accessed August 2021.

Phippen, A. (2016). *Children's online behaviour and safety: Policy and rights challenges.* Springer.

Phippen, A. (2021). *UK schools online safety policy & practice—Assessment 2021.* https://swgfl.org.uk/assets/documents/uk-schools-online-safety-policy-and-practice-assessment-2021.pdf. Accessed August 2021.

Phippen, A., & Brennan, M. (2019). *Child protection and safeguarding technologies: Appropriate or excessive 'solutions' to social problems?* Routledge.

Phippen, A., & Brennan, M. (2020). *Sexting and revenge pornography: Legislative and social dimensions of a modern digital phenomenon.* Routledge.

Setty, E. (2020). *Risk and harm in youth sexting: Young people's perspectives.* Routledge.

UK Government. (1978). *Section 1 Protection of Children Act 1978.* https://www.legislation.gov.uk/ukpga/1978/37/section/1. Accessed July 2021.

UK Government. (2015). *Section 33, Criminal Courts and Justice Act 2015.* https://www.legislation.gov.uk/ukpga/2015/2/section/33/enacted. Accessed August 2021.

UK Government. (2018). *Online harms white paper.* https://assets.publishing.service.gov.uk/government/uploads/system/uploads/attachment_data/file/793360/Online_Harms_White_Paper.pdf. Accessed August 2021.

UK Government. (2021). *Draft online safety bill 2021.* https://assets.publishing.service.gov.uk/government/uploads/system/uploads/attachment_data/file/985033/Draft_Online_Safety_Bill_Bookmarked.pdf. Accessed August 2021.

United Nations Human Rights Council. (2018). *Report of the Special Rapporteur on the promotion and protection of the right to freedom of opinion and expression.* https://documents-dds-ny.un.org/doc/UNDOC/GEN/G18/096/72/PDF/G1809672.pdf?OpenElement. Accessed August 2021.

Wikipedia. (n.d.). *The Scunthorpe problem.* https://en.wikipedia.org/wiki/Scunthorpe_problem. Accessed August 2021.

CHAPTER 3

Perennial Issues?

Abstract A personal reflection contrasts different aspects of youth work, comparing those with a preventative/prohibitive approach (such as online safety) against more progressive harm reduction approaches (such as drugs and alcohol awareness). Conversations with young people highlight that listening and supporting are more effective messages than "don't do it", and argue that resilience narratives are being hijacked by preventative agendas that, while new in the online safety world, have been prevalent in youth work for far longer.

Keywords Online safety · Digital resilience · Harm reduction · Youth work

In this chapter, I will outline some of the issues that have appeared over the last ten years for professionals working in the sector concerning young people's online activities. While not an exhaustive list, these are reflective of the major concerns professionals and parents/carers have about young people's online lives and draw extensively from my work with young people. It shows that the issues they face, and those that the adults in their lives fear, are often quite distinct.

The issues I will be outlining are:

© The Author(s), under exclusive license to Springer Nature Switzerland AG 2022
A. Phippen and L. Street, *Online Resilience and Wellbeing in Young People*, Palgrave Studies in Cyberpsychology,
https://doi.org/10.1007/978-3-030-88634-9_3

- Young people do not understand what resilience means.
- Professionals rely on a message of "just don't do it" due to a lack of capacity to explore issues in a more nuanced way.
- Professionals do not use harm reduction messages when it comes to online activities.
- Most adults believe playing violent video games leads to violent behaviour.
- Professionals and parents/carers fear that young people might access the "dark web" to buy drugs, when this is actually happening on social media.
- Adults do not know how to safeguard young people's rights when it comes to online activities.
- While young people may experience bullying online, they also find ways to access support and support one another online.

The chapter concludes with some reflections on how the need to develop support for professionals around these issues resulted in the research direction that resulted in the Online Resilience Tool.

Young People Do not Understand What Resilience Means

As a youth worker, I hear the word "resilience" everywhere. It is a concept that professionals working with young people are increasingly concerned about, and as a profession, we are constantly asking "How can we build resilience in young people?".

This question comes from a fundamentally good place, recognising that young people have to face challenges that didn't exist 10 years ago and that as professionals we don't necessarily have comparable personal experiences to draw on to support young people. As a result, schools, youth workers, social workers, police and parents/carers all talk to young people about resilience—we repeatedly tell them how important resilience is, but we never tell them specifically *what* it is.

In all the sessions I run with young people, I ask them what they understand by the word resilience. I've not had a correct definition to date. The suggested meanings are "you don't give up", "you keep going, no matter what", "you're brave" and, heartbreakingly, "you don't ask for help".

My definition is that resilience is the ability to bounce back when bad things happen, or.
as Masten puts it:

Resilience can be broadly defined as the capacity of a dynamic system to adapt successfully to disturbances that threaten system function, viability, or development. (Masten, 2014)

Definitions are really important when we think about how we talk to young people about Online Resilience. We should be taking great pains to ensure they understand what we mean when we talk about resilience. After all, we cannot completely insulate young people from bad things online. Nor should we be teaching them to just put up with bad things.

When these bad things are then reported to professionals, the ensuing panic surrounding the young person is likely to be something they dread, and may even be interpreted as a punishment.

I supported one young person who told me she had sent a nude to a boy in her year; he was then using this to blackmail and coerce her into sending more, under threat of revealing what she had done to her friends and family. When she told me, I explained that I had to tell someone in order to keep her safe. She begged me not to tell.

From her point of view, she was going to be in trouble for sending the photos. I explained the safeguarding process to her, following the rules I had learnt in training about not making promises that everything would be ok.

We were able to effectively safeguard the young person and prevent further exploitation from occurring on this occasion. However, the experience from her perspective was probably much what she predicted—her mum was angry at her for sending the picture in the first place and the police took her phone as part of their investigation.

Thinking of this example alone, we can see why young people would start to think that resilience means not telling people when things go wrong—keep your mouth shut and you'll be allowed the freedom to explore the online world, tell someone and you'll have your device and/or freedom to use that device, taken away, not to mention the negative/authoritative response from other adults. Again, general safeguarding training encourages professionals to consider their reaction when a young person discloses abuse, but parents/carers do not receive the same training, plus being highly emotionally invested in their child's happiness, they are likely to have their own feelings about harm coming to their child. Most parents/carers I have discussed these issues with are able to see that it's better to know what's happening, and therefore, an explosive reaction is unlikely to foster a positive atmosphere in which a young person can share mistakes they've made. However, the ability to rationalise this is quite different to applying it in practice.

It is precisely the experience of making mistakes that helps young people build their resilience, particularly in the context of the online world. Therefore, a better definition of resilience is this one:

> Digital resilience is a dynamic personality asset that grows from digital acti-vation i.e. through engaging with appropriate opportunities and challenges online, rather than through avoidance and safety behaviours. (UK Council for Internet Safety, 2019)

We need to give young people the tools to safely explore the online world, prepare them for it and support them when things go wrong—much like we do with the offline world. We need to recognise that a young person making a mistake once does not mean they are incapable of recognising all other online risks. Equally, a young person who shows a great deal of resilient behaviours in some areas will have others where they may be more likely to take risks or become vulnerable to grooming or harassment. We need to remember that resilience isn't fixed for young people, their ability to deal with challenges will vary based on their previous experience, personality type and culture (Masten, 2014).

A big problem with the way professionals have approached the issue of resilience and safety in the online world is that it is seen as an optional extra—both something professionals can choose whether or not to address (PSHE Association, 2020a) and something young people can choose to put down and walk away from.

However, since the 2020 lockdown, when schools began teaching lessons online, and the government rushed to ensure all pupils had access to devices for this purpose (Department for Education, 2020, 2021), the online world has not been an optional extra for young people. It has become a mandatory part of their education. As a result of lockdown, it's unsurprising that much social interaction moved online. While we're still waiting to see how much of "normality" we'll be getting back to, the ability of young people to walk away from the digital world has dwindled.

Additionally, professionals can no longer opt out of discussing the online world with young people as it is included in the, now mandatory, PSHE curriculum (Department for Education, 2019).

We must discuss Online Resilience with young people, before we reach the point of needing to safeguard them. We should accept that they will make mistakes, and be able to support them effectively when they do. We need to ensure they understand what we mean by resilience, and we need to ensure that we are not using "resilience" as a fixed thing which will either put them at risk or protect them in all circumstances.

Professionals Relying on "Just don't Do It" Messages Due to Lack of Capacity

I started my career as a youth worker in 2008, just as government cuts from austerity were starting to be felt across services. I've seen increasingly tight funding squeezed and stretched. I've seen traditional youth work approaches abandoned and many youth workers become disillusioned with the increasing volumes of paperwork required to prove the worth of the work they do with smaller and smaller budgets.

I've also seen thresholds increase, from mental health to sexual violence services; the only way statutory services could manage caseloads was to only deal with the most complex cases (Law et al., 2015). This hasn't solved anything, as workers are more likely to struggle with their own wellbeing as they manage the most complex cases, which in turn may not have become so complex had help been offered sooner (Merriman, 2017).

In a reaction to this, various pots of funding have been made available for preventative care, increasing the focus on "social prescribing" which aims to offer community support to people suffering with loneliness, weight gain and low mood (to name just a few) to prevent a later need for medical intervention. This is not with the goal of improving health and wellbeing, but specifically to reduce demand on healthcare services (Polley et al., 2017). Sadly, in my experience, this preventative care is often swallowed up by those people who don't quite meet thresholds for other services.

In one of my roles, I supported young people who were displaying high-risk sexual behaviour. This project was described as "Early Intervention", but many of the young people referred into the service had already experienced sexual violence, either as victim or as perpetrator.

As they weren't at risk of causing or experiencing immediate harm, they were ineligible for support from sexual violence services—much to the anguish of the parents/carers, social workers and teachers attempting to support them.

In many cases, I was working with young people who were actively engaged in high-risk activities, and often, the young person had refused to make any changes.

One young woman I supported had been told by her parents, teachers and social workers that she had to stop drinking and using drugs, because using substances with her peers had repeatedly put her in situations where she was unable to avoid sexual advances from other young people. She didn't think of what she had experienced as rape or sexual assault, and if she thought anyone was to blame, it was herself.

She had been preached at for several years about the dangers of drugs, told that drugs would kill her. She had been told about the long-term harms of alcohol use, the damage it would do to her liver and heart. She had been told about sex and STIs, but no one had ever talked seriously to her about the meaning of consent, nor the role that substances can play in our ability to consent. No one had talked to her about her right to access contraception. No one had talked to her about how having sex with someone once doesn't mean you consent to future sexual activity with that person. No one had told her that wearing a short skirt didn't mean she was responsible for the behaviour of the men around her.

The panic surrounding this young person, from her parents, school and social worker, was extreme. She had been reluctant to work with me and had only agreed on the basis that it would get these other professionals off her back.

It became clear to me that she had been repeatedly told to stop doing what she was doing, which to her reinforced the idea that any sexual assault or rape was her own fault. She was "putting herself at risk".

In the work I did with her, we explored how she could continue to go out and party but reduce the harm she experienced from using substances. This included being more selective of the friends she used around, and ensuring these friends knew what was ok for her and what wasn't, so they could help look after her. I also supported her to access contraception and talked at length about sexual pleasure and how she could ask for it from her sexual partners.

This might all seem like common sense to read—of course we should take a *harm reduction* approach if a young person is refusing to stop engaging in risky behaviour—but the interesting thing about this case is it wasn't one young woman. It was dozens of young women, all presenting in almost identical ways over several years.

These young women ranged in age from 14 to 17 and in many cases I had to break confidentiality to effectively safeguard these young women. Some of them needed specialist support from the young people's drug and alcohol service. Some needed mental health support. Some just needed a space to learn about sex without being told (explicitly or implicitly) not to do it.

It is certainly much more challenging to have a discussion about safer ways of using substances and how to seek sexual pleasure with a 14-year-old than a 17-year-old. However, we know that prohibitive messages are, at best, pointless and at worst can have effects opposite to their intention—we have seen it proven in studies into outcomes of the "just say no" approach to drugs (Werch & Owen, 2002). So why do we keep pedalling the prohibition message to young people?

Well, we've seen a massive increase in complexity and need which has to be managed with less money and less recognition (Law et al., 2015). As a practitioner in this profession, I've seen first-hand that the willingness to juggle this is motivated by a genuine desire to improve the welfare and future of young people.

Unfortunately, this means that young people who aren't actively engaged in risky or harmful behaviour are often left to their own devices (quite literally) save for a few blanket prohibitive messages. Despite all the evidence pointing to these messages being completely useless or counter-productive (Werch & Owen, 2002), I've seen them used all too often by over-stretched professionals as a quick and easy way to tick a box.

We're becoming stuck in a vicious circle of professionals with increasingly complex cases having less time to give to less complex young people. These young people therefore don't get appropriate and timely support, meaning they engage in more risky behaviours, leading them to become more complex if and when they eventually become eligible for support.

Another issue with prohibitive messages about online activities is that they can rarely be applied to the reality of using the internet. Take "don't give out your personal details on the internet". I was unsurprised that even the very youngest children we spoke to while conducting research in the Headstart Kernow project were able to parrot this message back to me. However, the frequent exceptions to this rule make it practically unhelpful as soon as young people have the freedom to use devices. I can't remember the last time I downloaded an app that didn't ask me for some sort of personal information—whether it's fitness apps that want to know everything about your body, or social media that require an email address in order to sign up—we constantly and willingly give out our personal information online.

Clearly, there are security issues with this, but we should be wary of trying to hold young people to a higher standard than adults. If we download these apps and give out our email address, phone number, height, weight, BMI and top 5 favourite films without a second thought, we are modelling behaviour to young people that they are likely to follow.

Telling young people to act differently to the behaviours we model might encourage them to follow rules when they are very young, but as soon as they reach adolescence they are likely to believe these rules no longer apply—which can lead to an increase in risk-taking if they perceive such behaviours to embody more "adult" activities (Morrongiello et al., 2008).

PROFESSIONALS DO NOT USE HARM REDUCTION MESSAGES

As a youth worker I know how useful short, snappy phrases can be to get a point across. "Start Low, Go Slow" is one of my favourites as it can be applied to any substance and is easy to remember. Thinking about taking ecstasy? Start low, go slow. More likely to use cannabis? Start low, go slow. It's a simple, memorable harm reduction message that even the most conservative professionals can see the benefits of.

The "Just Say No" approach to drug education was adopted in the UK in the 1980s, accompanied in 1987 by the eponymous song by the Grange Hill cast following a storyline about a young heroin user. The phrase was equally catchy and memorable. But was far less useful—once a young person had decided to use drugs, there was no further information about how to stay safe. By the early 1990s, harm reduction-based drug education emerged as a response, with grassroots approaches to getting safety messages about drugs out into the spaces where people were using drugs (Crew Scotland, 2018).

Persuading professionals to leave behind the seductive security of "Just Say No" has been a long journey, and with PSHE finally becoming mandatory in 2020 (PSHE Association, 2020b) the adoption of harm reduction techniques is finally becoming mainstream (PSHE Association, 2020a).

While this is great news, it has taken 40 years for sensible harm reduction information to be given to young people. Because drugs are illegal, it requires a body like the PSHE association to reassure professionals' reassurance that they won't fall foul of the law by talking to young people about how to take substances safely, as the end goal is to reduce harm from taking them. We also have to take sufficient time exploring the topic as a whole, discussing the nuances of the law and why we might tell young people about ways to reduce harm—this can't all be covered to the depth that young people deserve in one school assembly.

This same issue is currently being played out in another area of young people's online activity: that of sending nudes. As we have discussed in Chapter 2, the illegality of sending sexual messages is fairly well understood across all those working with young people, but the nuance of the law is not. Delivering training in Online Resilience to professionals, I've found a general lack of awareness that the law treats images and text differently, so if a 13-year-old sent a sexually explicit, text only message, they wouldn't be breaking the law. But if the message included a sexually explicit image, it would then be illegal.

In my experience, professionals have often expressed shock at this, which reveals a very simplistic understanding of how the digital world is used to express and explore sexuality and sexual behaviours.

Also, professionals tend to refer to this behaviour in young people as "sexting", which is unhelpful because it's not what young people call it. It's also unhelpful because the term is not commonly used to describe the same behaviour among adults. The problem with using the wrong word is that it draws a line between the lived experience of young people and the discussions we have in education settings to attempt to help them recognise risks and stay safe.

In my role working for a sex education charity, one of the most popular activities in sex education sessions was to get the young people to call out all the different names they knew for penis and vulva. This led to much hilarity as groups of young people would try to come up with the most obscure (and often obscene) names they could think of. But there was a serious side to this activity, and that was to ensure we were all talking about the same thing.

When we refer to "sexting" rather than to nudes, dick pics, tit pics, etc., we invent a behaviour which we, as adults, probably don't identify with and which the young people are unlikely to identify with either. Sexting is tied up with the legality of sending sexual messages. It's not linked to the desire to share images that may excite or interest a potential sexual partner for mutual (or sometimes not mutual) sexual gratification. Young people aren't sending nudes because they don't understand the risks of doing so (and in the next chapter I'll explore what their understanding of those risks are); they're sending nudes because they want to get themselves, or someone else, off (Symons et al., 2018).

Then, there is the moral panic around "sexting". An NSPCC survey in 2016 showed that "7% of 11–16 year olds surveyed had shared a naked or semi naked image of themselves" (NSPCC, 2016). However, a YouGov survey from the same year found that 78% of parents were "either fairly or very concerned about sexting" (PSHE Association, 2016).

From this, we can see that there is a great deal of fear around the idea of sending nudes and yet our approaches to talking to young people about it focus on the idea that it's an abnormal behaviour and suggest young people will only do it when pressured into doing so. This is the message from the Childnet teaching resources (Childnet International, 2018) which are currently recommended by the PSHE Association (PSHE Association, 2019).

I'm not suggesting we shouldn't be teaching young people about the risks of sending these images, nor that we shouldn't be telling them that to do so is illegal. But a reliance on this message alone is likely to be as (un)successful as "Just Say No".

We need to tell young people about the risks of sending these messages in a context that will be meaningful to them. That does need to include teaching them about what might happen if those images are shared beyond the intended recipient—which should also include a discussion of how to get help if that happens—but our discussion must go beyond that.

Telling young people "if you send this message you'll lose control of it and it could be used to trick, humiliate or coerce you, plus you're breaking the law if you send it" is the same message as "if you take ecstasy you'll die in hospital, plus you're breaking the law by having it in the first place". Young people can plainly see that not everyone who takes ecstasy dies or gets arrested, and they can see just as clearly that not every nude gets publicly leaked, and not everyone who sends one gets arrested.

Not all young people will send nudes, but all young people need to understand that there are risks to doing so. We should be myth busting how many young people actually do this, exploring how young people can manage these risks *if* they choose to send nudes and where they can get help if something goes wrong. We need the equivalent of a "Start Low, Go Slow" message for sending nudes.

It's also important to note that the consensual sharing of sexual images is not the same as young people being groomed or exploited online (Symons et al., 2018). It is extremely important that young people are taught to recognise when someone is pressuring them to send an image, but we cannot continue to lump the appalling exploitation of children in with their own, normal explorations of their sexuality. We need to stop teaching these two distinct experiences as one and the same thing, much as we would not teach how to negotiate sexual activity with a partner in the same breath as sexual abuse.

However, while young people can be criminalised for taking and sending sexually explicit images of themselves, it's going to be extremely difficult to effectively encourage them to get help. While Outcome 21 allows for "no formal criminal justice action to be taken", the incident is still recorded and therefore may show up on future DBS checks (Avon and Somerset Police, 2021). Until we can reassure victims that they will not be criminalised, we are going to struggle to effectively encourage young people to talk to us if they have had an image shared on without consent, or have been pressured or coerced into sending more images.

Not only does this situation look set to continue for the foreseeable future, but the same rules are starting to be applied across more situations; for example, hate speech on social media may be returned on a DBS check, even if it's recorded as a non-crime hate incident (Lyons, 2021).

Violent Video Games Lead to Violent Behaviour?

As we have illustrated at the commencement of this book, there is a strong, and unsubstantiated view among professionals working with young people that playing violent video games leads to violent behaviour. Instances of gunmen who attacked their school having played violent video games are used to illustrate this, and very little additional thought is put into it (strangely, eating crisps and pizza are never explored as common denominators in these cases, yet they must be as likely to yield positive results?). Longitudinal studies show no increase in violence linked to video game sales and increase in aggression is not apparent in the medium to long term (Cunningham et al., 2016).

Certainly, part of the problem is with the way professionals and parents/carers view the issue. If a child is playing a computer game and loses, or their internet connection drops out, or someone turns off their console, they're likely to have an aggressive response. This proves the belief that violent video games lead to violent behaviours. Obviously, it doesn't prove that, but those professionals and parents/carers are unlikely to consider the child's longer-term record which may show a lack of violent behaviours.

THE DARK WEB

In all my conversations with professionals about young people buying drugs online, the most common belief is that young people are using the dark web to do it. Perhaps this comes from a lack of understanding about what the dark web is. I don't think this is an adequate excuse. If a professional was supporting a young person who loved football, we would expect them to find out about football, at least enough to engage with the young person on the subject. However, commonly professionals and parents/carers will say "I don't know anything about computers/social media/technology" as though this exempts them from learning enough about it to discuss it with young people.

While there are inevitably some young people using the dark web to buy drugs, the majority of young people will have experienced a dealer trying to add them on social media. Speaking to a group of young people on the subject, one young woman explained that when it's coming up to a birthday or big event, dealers will send young people direct messages, knowing that they'll be looking to party. This is supported by the DM for Details report by Volteface, which explains that the sale of drugs on social media is not a simple re-creation of the offline drugs market, but an entirely new sales model (McCulloch & Furlong, 2019).

This disconnect between what professionals and parents/carers believe and what is actually happening again creates issues for having meaningful discussions with young people about the online risks they may be facing.

In the time that adults have been panicking about young people using the dark web, drug dealers have developed new approaches to selling on social media, including ways to get around the platform's filtering, for example by having a photograph of a page with a menu of available drugs, but an innocuous caption unrelated to drugs (Volteface, 2019).

The risks of buying drugs on social media are actually somewhat greater than buying drugs on the dark web. There are harm reduction practices that can be used when buying drugs on the dark web, for example reading reviews (which can't be deleted by the seller on most dark markets) and only buying from sellers who have lots of very recent reviews (Volteface, 2019). Social media can offer none of these assurances. Dealer accounts are likely to appear and disappear extremely swiftly and reviews can be made up and deleted by the account holder. Therefore, it's impossible to get a sense of the quality of the product before purchasing.

Additionally, dealers are targeting young people because they are looking for inexperienced customers—in my work with young people around substances, I've seen drugs sold in this way which have little or none of the substance they are sold as with prices which are higher than their general market value.

While we cannot and should not expect professionals to keep up to date with every possible risk young people may face on social media, let alone the abundance of platforms and apps they may be using, there is a need for some common myth busting to help professionals and parents/carers have relevant discussions with young people about risks such as these.

Safeguarding Young People's Rights

The UN Convention on the Rights of the Child (UNCRC) is the standard to which all those working with young people are expected to adhere. It is taught as part of safeguarding training and is referenced in everything from funding bids to youth clubs. This proliferation means that most professionals working with young people will have some experience of applying the rights listed in the convention to their real world, lived experience of work.

Within the digital world, however, the understanding and application of these rights are often poorly understood. The right covered by the UNCRC that professionals seem to struggle with the most in terms of young people's online activities though is the Right to Privacy (United Nations, 1989).

Interestingly, the young people we spoke to in the course of developing the tool had a very clear understanding of their right to privacy, at least from the eyes of their parents/carers, if not from wider institutions that would like to gather their data (Livingstone et al., 2018). In a discussion with a group of 8- to 12-year-olds, the children were able to clearly articulate that they felt they should be allowed to keep messages to their friends private, because their parents/carers were able to do the same thing.

In the offline world, a child of this age would expect to spend time with their friends outside of the earshot of parents/carers. If they found a parent listening at their bedroom door, they would be upset and angry at this invasion of privacy. And yet parents/carers and professionals are often told that in order to protect children, we must track their online activities. This is promoted as essential for their safe development; however, the evidence is quite the opposite, and preventing children from exploring both on and offline can inhibit their development (Livingstone et al., 2018).

Talking to parents/carers of younger children, the complexity of this is apparent. We do not want children to be playing, unsupervised online—much as we would not want them left in the park unsupervised. But what do we mean when we talk about children's privacy?

Nissembaum defines privacy as "neither a right to secrecy nor a right to control, but a right to appropriate flow of personal information" (cited in Livingstone et al., 2018, 12). This helps us to navigate these murky waters.

We need to ensure children and young people know what supervision and oversight their parents/carers have over their online activities—and *why*—so that they are informed of the flow of information and can make informed decisions about what they do with it.

Managing the right to privacy is going to vary widely from the youngest age group up to the oldest. While an 8-year-old may accept that their parent/carer will read their messages from time to time, a 15-year-old is unlikely to accept the same treatment. Parents/carers may need advice from professionals about how to manage this. Unfortunately again, professionals' lack of confidence in this area is likely to interfere with their ability to appropriately offer this advice. Many professionals have asked me what tracking software they should recommend, what apps that limit internet usage are the best and how parents/carers can bypass a young person's password on a device.

These questions fundamentally undermine the right to privacy, and there are many apps that are willing to take parent's money with shady promises of "keeping young people safe".

I cannot stress how important it is to have conversations with young people about their online activities. If parents/carers use apps such as "Find My..." this should be discussed with the young person. Parents/carers should also be aware that young people can stop sharing their location if they wish, and that in reality these apps can only tell them the location of a device, not a young person. It doesn't require much cunning for a young person to realise that if they leave their phone with a friend, they can then roam around in places they are not meant to be without fearing the consequences. But we *should* fear the consequences of making young people so wary of being tracked that they decide to go somewhere risky without a way of calling for help.

If a parent/carer decides to track their young person's phone, or installs software enabling them to read messages, etc., even if this is done with the young person's knowledge, this should still be negotiable. If the young person is 13 and the parents/carers have reason to believe they may be facing or taking unacceptably high levels of risk it may be appropriate for parents/carers to set up location sharing and have rules about oversight of messages. But if the young person is 16 and has started a consensual sexual relationship with a peer, and has shown a responsible attitude to their sexual health, it would be highly inappropriate for parents/carers to continue monitoring their device.

EXPERIENCING ONLINE ABUSE AND GETTING SUPPORT

Professionals and parents/carers have long been concerned about "cyberbullying". Reports of young people experiencing bullying online are often deeply disturbing, as the harassment is constantly with them—they do not get a reprieve when they leave school or college as they likely have a device with them at all times.

However, in the fear around online bullying, there is often a missed discussion about how young people can support one another online.

We get lost in the myriad risks and problems the online world causes in young people's lives and fail to see the benefits young people may experience from accessing online support.

I have seen young people access online support groups for issues as diverse as eating disorders, gender dysphoria and autism. These young people may find that there are no other young people near them with similar issues, particularly in a rural county like Cornwall where groups that support, for example, transgender young people are often county-wide and may be difficult for young people to access with the support of a parent for transport.

These online support groups can offer a sense of belonging to young people, which is an especially strong driver in adolescence (Harris, 2013).

There are, of course, positives and negatives to online support groups. The positives include the lack of geographical or time boundaries (meaning people in different countries and time zones can connect to support one another), the ability to be anonymous—giving people the freedom to discuss issues with less fear of judgement and the ability to share experiences. The negatives include the possible "digital divide" (meaning those without access to the internet are further disadvantaged), lack of appropriate boundaries and the possibility of shared information being inaccurate (Kirk & Milnes, 2016). I have seen, for many of the young people I have supported, the positives may outweigh the negatives in cases where they feel unable to talk to friends or parents/carers about their concerns.

A great example of this is a trend which emerged on social media sites in 2020 of people talking about "finishing their shampoo and conditioner at the same time". I received a somewhat panicked email which had been circulated to hundreds (if not thousands) of professionals in Cornwall working with young people. The Blue Whale Challenge scare had just reared its head again, and this email explained that young people who say they had pasta for tea, or had finished their shampoo and conditioner at the same time, were using code to say they were feeling suicidal.

This isn't uncommon in youth work settings. Professionals often share information to help others decode the complex language young people use. However, this time I felt sad and frustrated that the whole point of this trend had been missed.

The idea came from a beautiful poem by Hannah Dains called "Don't Kill Yourself Today" (Dains, 2015), which had been going around on various social media platforms for a couple of years by the time the email landed in my inbox. I hadn't seen the trend on TikTok, but I had heard the poem, and knew immediately that this was likely the source of the trend.

When young people posted about this online, they would receive supportive, positive messages from people who understood (Tempesta, 2020), they understood because you would have to have an interest in mental wellbeing for the poem to show up on your feed, and therefore, it was a way of asking for help from an already supportive audience.

Similarly, I have supported young people with eating disorders who have accessed pro-ana (pro-anorexia) websites initially as part of their disorder, but who have then continued to access these sites when they were in recovery as a way of reaching out to other young people who are experiencing the same issues they were.

Professionals may have a limited understanding of the support young people access online and are also likely to be relatively unaware of the risks. It is not enough to share information saying that if a young person talks about finishing their shampoo and conditioner at the same time they may be feeling suicidal, we need to have an understanding of what these memes *mean* to young people and what support they may be receiving through platforms professionals may only associate with risk.

In order to support young people, it's vital that professionals and parents/carers do not stop at the first question. Online support can be wonderful, or it can be extremely risky. We can only learn which it is through talking to young people about it. This should include talking about the risks and the benefits, as well as managing those risks, and how we can support them to do so.

Conclusion

In this chapter, I have outlined some of the emerging issues young people face in their online lives. It is apparent that adults are often stuck using outdated or overly simplistic messages in an effort to keep young people safe. We need to move professionals and parents/carers on from these, giving them confidence to explore the issues with young people without being bamboozled by the technology. There is also a need to have clear messaging on which behaviours constitute high risk to young people, and which do not. It was this need that led to the development of the Online Resilience Tool. In the next chapter, we will start to explore the findings of the Headstart Kernow project, and how it fed into the development of the tool.

REFERENCES

Avon and Somerset Police. (2021). *Sexting*. Avon and Somerset Police. https://www.avonandsomerset.police.uk/crime-prevention-advice/sexting/. Accessed August 2021.

Childnet International. (2018). *"Sexting"* —*Just send it*. Childnet International. https://www.childnet.com/resources/pshe-toolkit/crossing-the-line/sexting. Accessed August 2021.

Crew Scotland. (2018). *Origins*. Crew Scotland. https://www.crew.scot/who-we-are/origins/. Accessed August 2021.

Cunningham, S., Engelstätter, B., & Ward, M. (2016). Violent video games and violent crime. *Southern Economic Journal, 82*(4), 1247–1265. https://doi.org/10.1002/soej.12139

Dains, H. (2015). *Don't kill yourself today* [Spoken Word Poetry]. YouTube. https://www.youtube.com/watch?v=-Ktdf2KQ58c. Accessed August 2021.

Department for Education. (2019). *Relationships education, relationships and sex education (RSE) and health education*. gov.uk. https://assets.publishing.service.gov.uk/government/uploads/system/uploads/attachment_data/file/908013/Relationships_Education__Relationships_and_Sex_Education__RSE__and_Health_Education.pdf. Accessed August 2021.

Department for Education. (2020). *Get laptops and tablets for pupils and students who cannot access face-to-face education due to coronavirus (COVID-19)*. gov.uk. https://www.gov.uk/guidance/get-laptops-and-tablets-for-children-who-cannot-attend-school-due-to-coronavirus-covid-19#more-laptops-and-tablets-will-be-available-in-2021. Accessed August 2021.

Department for Education. (2021). *Remote education good practice*. gov.uk. Retrieved April 14, 2021 from https://www.gov.uk/government/publications/remote-education-good-practice/remote-education-good-practice. Accessed August 2021.

Harris, P. (2013). *Youthoria*. Russel House Publishing.

Kirk, S., & Milnes, L. (2016). An exploration of how young people and parents use online support in the context of living with cystic fibrosis. *Health Expectations, 19*(2), 309–321. https://doi.org/10.1111/hex.12352

Law, D., Faulconbridge, J., & Laffan, A. (2015). How big an issue is children and young people's mental health? *The Child & Family Clinical Psychology Review, 3*, 8–11. https://www.researchgate.net/profile/Duncan-Law/publication/283634680_What_good_looks_like_in_psychological_services_for_children_young_people_and_their_families_special_edition_of_the_child_and_family_clinical_psychology_review/links/5641c1e308ae24cd3e426. Accessed August 2021.

Livingstone, S., Stoilova, M., & Nandagiri, R. (2018). Children's data and privacy online, an evidence review. *LSE Media & Communication*. https://www.lse.ac.uk/media-and-communications/assets/documents/research/pro

jects/childrens-privacy-online/Evidence-review-final.pdf. Accessed August 2021.

Lyons, I. (2021). *Children warned future careers could be ruined by old tweets. The Telegraph.* https://www.telegraph.co.uk/news/2021/04/05/children-warned-future-careers-could-ruined-old-tweets/. Accessed August 2021.

Masten, A. S. (2014). Global perspectives on resilience in children and youth. *Child Development, 85*(1), 6–20. https://srcd.onlinelibrary.wiley.com/doi/pdfdirect/10.1111/cdev.12205

McCulloch, L., & Furlong, S. (2019). *DM for details. Selling drugs in the age of social media.* Volteface. https://volteface.me/app/uploads/2020/08/Volteface-_-Social-Media-report-DM-for-Details.pdf. Accessed August 2021.

Merriman, J. C. (2017). *Burnout in mental health professionals: The role of individual characteristics.* University of Southampton. https://eprints.soton.ac.uk/425914/. Accessed August 2021.

Morrongiello, B. A., Corbett, M., & Bellissimo, A. (2008). "Do as I say, not as I do": Family influences on children's safety and risk behaviors. *Health Psychology, 27*(4), 498–503.

NSPCC. (2016). *I wasn't sure it was normal to watch it.* NSPCC. https://learning.nspcc.org.uk/research-resources/2016/i-wasn-t-sure-it-was-normal-to-watch-it. Accessed August 2021.

Polley, M., Bertotti, M., Kimberlee, R., Pilkington, K., & Refsum, C. (2017). *A review of the evidence assessing impact of social prescribing on healthcare demand and cost implications.* University of Westminster. https://westminsterresearch.westminster.ac.uk/download/e18716e6c96cc93153baa8e757f8feb602fe99539fa281433535f89af85fb550/297582/review-of-evidence-assessing-impact-of-social-prescribing.pdf. Accessed August 2021.

PSHE Association. (2016). *Parents call for education to address sexting by children and young people.* PSHE Association. https://www.pshe-association.org.uk/news/parents-call-education-address-sexting-children. Accessed August 2021.

PSHE Association. (2019). *Childnet 'crossing the line' online safety PSHE toolkit.* PSHE Association. https://www.pshe-association.org.uk/curriculum-and-resources/resources/childnet-crossing-line-online-safety-pshe-toolkit. Accessed August 2021.

PSHE Association. (2020a). *Drug and alcohol education—Lesson plans, resources & knowledge organisers.* PSHE Association. https://www.pshe-association.org.uk/curriculum-and-resources/resources/drug-and-alcohol-education-%E2%80%94-lesson-plans. Accessed August 2021.

PSHE Association. (2020b). *The long road to statutory PSHE education (almost!).* PSHE Association. https://www.pshe-association.org.uk/long-road-statutory-pshe-education-almost. Accessed August 2021.

Symons, K., Ponnet, K., Walrave, M., & Heirman, W. (2018). Sexting scripts in adolescent relationships: Is sexting becoming the norm? *New Media & Society, 20*, 3836–3857. https://doi.org/10.1177/1461444818761869

Tempesta, E. (2020). *Is your teen secretly struggling with depression? How Gen Z is using the secret code 'I had pasta tonight' as a cry for help on social media when they are feeling depressed or suicidal.* Mail Online. https://www.dailymail.co.uk/femail/article-8476875/How-teens-using-code-pasta-tonight-reveal-depression.html. Accessed August 2021.

UK Council for Internet Safety. (2019). *Digital resilience framework.* UKCIS. https://www.gov.uk/government/publications/digital-resilience-framework. Accessed August 2021.

United Nations. (1989). *UN convention on the rights of the child.* Unicef. https://downloads.unicef.org.uk/wp-content/uploads/2016/08/unicef-convention-rights-child-uncrc.pdf. Accessed August 2021.

Volteface. (2019). *DM for details* [Podcast]. The Volteface Podcast.

Werch, C. E., & Owen, D. M. (2002). Iatrogenic effects of alcohol and drug prevention programs. *Journal of Studies on Alcohol, 63*(5), 581–590. https://doi.org/10.15288/jsa.2002.63.581

CHAPTER 4

Listening to Young People's Concerns

Abstract Much policy and debate in the online safeguarding world are driven by adultist views and a lack of youth voice. The Headstart Kernow project adopted an entirely flipped approach to researching how to support young people who had been subject to online harms by starting with a blank page and having the focus any intervention being driven by a youth voice. Underpinned with trauma-informed approaches, which are now prevalent in the children's mental health arena, we argue that the lack of consideration of digital issues among adverse childhood experiences presents challenges when applying this approach to online safeguarding. What became clear from the work was that there was a prevailing view that adults will overreact to disclosures or not understand what they were told, and therefore, there was no point in disclosing. The discussions with young people were wide ranging and illustrated that many adultist concerns were not aligned with the reality of youth interactions online.

Keywords Online safety · Digital resilience · Adverse childhood experiences · Trauma-informed schools

By way of contrast to the policy analysis in Chapter 2, this chapter presents the initial discussions with young people to better understand their concerns about digital technology and whether the current approaches

© The Author(s), under exclusive license to Springer Nature
Switzerland AG 2022
A. Phippen and L. Street, *Online Resilience and Wellbeing in Young
People*, Palgrave Studies in Cyberpsychology,
https://doi.org/10.1007/978-3-030-88634-9_4

in their education experiences were effective. Developing on observations from Chapter 3, and based upon extensive focus group activity with over 100 children and young people, this chapter examines some fundamental questions juxtaposing the policy perspective with young people's own views around what actually causes upset online, the data from which demonstrates a breadth of issues that cannot easily be addressed through technical countermeasures.

A lot of young people's "online harms" centre on peer abuse, communication issues and a broad range of "upsetting" content, rather than the more adultist perspective that harms are done *to* young people, rather than *by* them. Another key facet of these early explorations centred on the knowledge of those with caring responsibilities, whether parents, teachers, or other safeguarding professionals. It was clear from our discussions that most young people had little confidence in adult's knowledge of the online world, or how concerns and harms can be tackled. Most young people's educational experiences involved little more than being shown videos in large class scenarios, with no opportunity to discuss. Others stated that adults would exaggerate potential harms and dismiss young people's concerns with prohibitive messages such as "you shouldn't be doing that" or "you've only got yourselves to blame". Clearly, when considering how we develop resilience among young people, a lack of support from adults is a significant concern.

In this chapter, we also explore the research methodology and development process for this resource; the tool was a cumulation of three years research with young people and those working with young people and, we hope, ultimately provides support for those working in the children's workforce to make a more nuanced and informed decisions and to provide individual support for young people who might disclose issues around their use of digital technology. Once the tool was defined in a form agreed by the project research team, it was then validated with focus groups with young people and carers, to ensure behaviours were effectively defined and categorised, which is discussed in Chapter 5.

Digital Research in Headstart Kernow

Returning to the goals of the Headstart Kernow work, as one would anticipated with the formation of a project that considers practice around children's mental health, there was a lot of workshops and discussions with professional teams to bring in their observations and expertise in considering what project goals might be and the outcomes they wanted from the project.

What was clear from these discussions, drawn mainly from a project steering board comprising senior education, social care and public health professionals, "online" was definitely an issue and often seen as the driver for wellbeing and mental health issues. The prevailing view seemed to be that issues such as sexting, cyberbullying and online screen time were all causal factors in wellbeing issues and preventative approaches. What was less clear was evidence to support these concerns. When pushed on evidence of these issues, it was clear most professionals had received no training on online safeguarding and we bring views from the media into these professional discussions. It was also very clear, even at these early stages of discussion, that there was a gulf between professional opinion and young people's experiences.

While professionals would generally adopt as preventative position (e.g. "how do we stop young people from sexting"), young people would acknowledge that online issues play a part in their wellbeing, but would balance negatives with positives and look to adults to support them if something went wrong. They do not want a *digital white knight* preventing harm from occurring, they want advice and support. What was clear from early discussions with young people (discussed in this chapter) is that you could not prevent issues occurring online just as you could not prevent verbal abuse or harassment in an offline setting. However, there was an expectation that adults should know how to support them in the event of harm or concern as a result of an online issue.

Adverse Childhood Experiences

The project as a whole adopted a *Trauma-Informed Schools* approach to considering children's mental health and wellbeing. This is now a well-established (e.g. Walkley & Cox, 2013) whole school approach acknowledging that a child who has experienced trauma is more likely to experience behavioural and learning challenges in schools. While trauma-informed approaches vary a great deal, what lies at the heart of these approaches is to acknowledge trauma has a long-term impact on mental health and wellbeing and early intervention is more effective than intervention once a young person is presenting serious mental health concerns. There is a view that schools are an ideal place for early intervention (see Chafouleas et al., 2016) due to the amount of time a young person spends in a school setting and the likelihood that early signs of mental health concern could be identified by the professionals who work there.

While this book is not a broad exploration of trauma-informed school approaches, it is worthwhile to consider the underlying empirical evidence as it informed what became a highly participative and ethnographic approach to exploring the role of digital technology on young people's wellbeing and how they might be best supported in navigated growing up in a connected world.

At the foundations of trauma-informed approaches is the now well-established concept of Adverse Childhood Experiences (Fellitti et al., 1998) (ACEs). Considerable evidence now exists to demonstrate that early childhood experiences can have a significant impact on life course and future wellbeing. There is a wealth of research that shows clear causation (e.g. see Kalmakis & Chandler, 2015) for these effects, and the findings of studies are now well embedded into practice.

Broadly speaking, Adverse Childhood Experiences are things the young person is subjected to themselves, and environmental factors, and can be separated into three categories:

Abuse:

    Sexual abuse
    Verbal abuse
    Physical abuse

Neglect:

    Physical neglect
    Emotional neglect

Household Dysfunction:

    Incarceration
    Substance abuse
    Mental illness
    Parental separation
    Domestic abuse

While others have been identified in further studies (e.g. Pachter et al., 2017), the focus remains on either environment factors or harms to the young person.

When we are considering the impact of technologically facilitated behaviours on young people's wellbeing, the definition of ACEs presents us with a fundamental issue, and one with which we were highly cognisant during the early stages of the project. While a trauma-informed approach, with a knowledge of ACEs, is a worthy foundation for a project that aimed to address early intervention and cross-sector mental health support for young people, the underlying knowledge base had scant consideration of how online issues might impact upon children's mental health.

While there are two ACEs defined that may manifest through online technology—sexual abuse (sometimes referred to as online non-contact abuse when occurring digitally) and verbal abuse—there is little discussion in the literature that has explored whether online issues might impact upon wellbeing or the sort of causation explored in the original ACE study. This is not a surprise, given that the methodology for the identification of ACEs is surveying adults about experiences as a child. Clearly we are not sufficiently advanced in the digital world (consider Facebook was only established in 2004, Instagram in 2010 and SnapChat in 2011) that adults can reflect back upon potential adverse impacts as a result of online harms.

That is not to say that there is no evidence related to children's use of digital technology and its harm (see Livingstone et al., 2017 for a detailed review). However, the majority of this research focussed upon trying to quantify harm and explore behaviour, rather than considering the more complex trauma that might occur and impact upon mental health or future life, as we will discuss below. While if we reflect on widely reported media stories about mental health concerns (e.g. GambleAware, 2019; Royal College of Psychiatrist, 2020; The World Health Organisation, 2019), the evidence base to underpin these views is scant. Indeed, an analysis across a large dataset on young people's mental health by the Oxford Internet Institute (Orben & Przybylski, 2019) showed there is little to suggest causation and there is greater impact on a young person's mental health from missing a meal than spending a long time online.

The Digital Resilience Workpackage in the Headstart Kernow Project

Therefore, from the early stages of the project, we took the view we would not assume the impact of digital technology, or more correctly the use of digital technology, on children and young people's mental health we would, instead, speak to them about it and, adopt a fundamental principle of the Headstart Kernow project, be driven by the youth voice from the outset.

The digital workstream on the Headstart Kernow project was established to explore young people's use and attitudes towards digital technology with a youth perspective from the ground up. We placed a condition at the start of the programme that we would not be led by policy agendas and would instead take a grounded theory approach in that we would learn from data collection. We were clear there was very little credible literature to support the assumptions that there *must* be a negative impact, and history shows us the same assumptions have been applied to video games, television, radio and books (Mueller, 2019) and can be linked back to Cohen's (2011)'s work on moral panics, which has previously been explored alongside digital harm narratives (Phippen & Bond, 2020). We therefore took the position we did not actually know what the impact of digital technology is on young people's wellbeing and the best people to explore this with are young people themselves.

In our observations, young people tend to be "early adopters" on emerging technology and will use technology in a manner most adults will not. They will explore, navigate and interact in a far more open and risk-free manner than many older users. This sometimes creates a cultural tension where adults do not understand the young people's behaviour and therefore assume it must be bad. While young people are, in general, engaged with technology, their capabilities, appreciation of risk and approaches to addressing concerns vary greatly. These terms come from adultist perspectives on childhood where the needs of the individual are reduced in favour of uniform educative messages such as "don't go online until you're, it's illegal" or "if you share something online and it goes further, you only have yourself to blame".

We would not, however, wish to adopt the problematic discourse around "Digital Natives". This is one term we come across frequently in the evolution of online safeguarding discourse over the last fifteen years. Coined by Prensky (2001), as a phrase differentiating between children—*digital natives*—and adults—*digital immigrants*—the concept rapidly found into way into academic and educational discourse.

Prensky's Digital Native idea comes from an article that proposes a theory where because someone was born in an era where digital technology was ubiquitous, they had some inbuilt ability to engage with it with capabilities that are missing from previous generations generalised as digital immigrants. While this crude generalisation is now widely debunked (e.g. Helsper & Eynon, 2010), its use still pervades in popular discourse.

We have certainly attended seminars and workshops around digital literacies and safeguarding where senior speakers from government and regulators have unhelpfully spoken of younger generations being natives capable of navigating the digital world without further support. To paraphrase one professional in a training session:

> They know more than me because they're a digital native, it comes naturally to them.

The term, when unchallenged, has become a taken-for-granted assumption and we frequently hear it from all manner of professionals, mainly used in one of two ways—firstly, as a way to imply blame:

> They're digital natives, they should know about this sort of thing

Or it is used to deflect responsibility:

> I'm not a digital native like they are, they know more than me.

Brown and Czerniewicz (2010) among others are also highly critical of the concept as such terminology hides inequalities in digital experiences. Furthermore, given that *Digital Native* ties in with the concept of *Millennials* (born between mid-1980s and early 2000s) and *Generation Z* (late 1990s—approximately 2015), this is not a term that could simply be applied to children and young people now—it is both unproven and now obsolete when we are concerned with the online safeguarding of young people in 2021. If we were to engage with this many adults would now be considered digital natives, including some who are claiming there are cultural challenges in online safeguarding because young people are *now* digital natives.

Returning to the young man who showed evidence of wisdom beyond his years in stating "what do you mean by safe anyway?", this was something we were mindful of throughout this work. This view, shared by lots of other young people we have spoken to (and which we will explore in more detail below), formed the basis on the tool—we can't make young people safe, but we can work at helping them become more resilient.

One doesn't become resilient by being excluded from something, one becomes resilient by understanding risk and where support is available. Moreover, and arguably more importantly, people with safeguarding responsibilities have a greater chance of being able to provide that support that young people are talking about if they are well informed on the nature of digital risk, and the severity of the risk (or whether there should be concern at all). To paraphrase a 12-year-old young woman from a different session, when asked what they felt online safety should be, she said:

> That you know who you can talk to when you're upset by something that has happened online, and that they can help you.

We did not wish to define the "definitive" resource to any aspect of youth online behaviour, as this would be impossible. We wish, instead, to develop a resource that would allow professionals to make more informed decisions about how to support young people, working alongside their existing safeguarding policies and training, and try to bridge the gap between preventative perspectives from adults (driven by biases and a dearth of training) and a wish for help and support by young people (a wish unfulfilled as a result of not wishing to disclose and risk the wrath of an adult).

Drawing from Discussions with Young People

The research work with young people, which ultimately resulted in the development of the Online Resilience Tool, was built upon a great deal of interaction with young people during the first three years of the programme.

Prior to the commencement of the main phase of the research project, we ran a pilot study to gain some grounding in young people's views. This took the form of an exploratory workshop with KS4 students from 4 schools, where they were initially encouraged to post up general opinions on the statement "digital technology has a negative impact young people's lives" on flip charts around the room, prior to engaging in smaller group discussions facilitated by Headstart staff, including ourselves.

While this was a short (2 h) session with around 100 young people from year 10 (aged 14–15), it allowed us to lay the foundations of our understanding of young people's views on the online safeguarding education and how they are supported by adults. We saw a frustration by young people with the nature of online safety they receive and a feeling that their views were dismissed because "adults think they know best". However, this was often caveated with a view by the young people "even though adults really did not". There was a clear view among young people that while digital technology was essentially a positive aspect in their lives, there were some things where it could cause upset and harm, for example receiving abuse or seeing upsetting content. However, they were unlikely to speak to adults about this because they anticipated a negative response in general.

However, perhaps more telling was the behaviour of professionals at the workshop. Young people were brought together from four different schools and, as one would expect, teaching staff came with them. Aside from one school, where the two teachers immediately sat on tables with the young people in the discussion group area, the other staff all placed their students on their respective tables and then departed to the back of the room to chat among themselves.

They did not view this discussion as something they needed to be part of and saw it as an opportunity to get on with work away from the students. Perhaps this is an unfair observation, and the teachers did not know they were invited to take part in the discussions. However, it is something we have experienced in other work activities—sometimes teachers will join in with discussions, sometimes they will sit at the back of the room doing marking, sometimes they will go "you're alright here aren't you?" and disappear to the staff room. It is notable that for the group where the teachers immediately sat with the students, this was the group where the young people were more open about their views on the online safety education they received in schools, and were more likely to disclose upset and harm.

Nevertheless, those staff who did disappear to the back of the room were invited to the discussion. Some engaged positively, some less so. However, one member of staff made a point of telling us afterwards that they had "learned so much" from listening to their students about their online lives.

The pilot study changed our outlook significantly—while initially we were of the view that we might develop resources to help young people better appreciate the impact of online behaviours upon their wellbeing, we decided to consider instead focussing any outcomes from the research on a tool for professionals. Even in the early stages of the research, it was clear that the young people were overloaded with resources, whereas professionals made decisions without any support. A decision was made, therefore, to focus on the goal of the workstream on developing practical resource, underpinned by all of our discussions with young people, that would be of sound practical help for those in the children's workforce who are making safeguarding judgements.

In this pilot group that the issue was not the activities young people were doing online (which was mainly positive), it was the lack of support, or overreaction by professionals, when harm was disclosed. If we could develop something that might help professionals we might result in an environment where better support was provided to young people who were truly exhibiting problematic behaviours, and lessen overreactions for those engaged in misunderstood activities.

Embarking on the research study proper, which took place over two years in the early stages of the Headstart Kernow project, we maintained an open, exploratory approach to the discussion with young people.

Dialogue with young people took place in a number of different ways, but always in school settings. Approaches to discussion included:

- Large workshops drawing young people from different schools with facilitated discussion (attendance was around 60 students in each case).
- Discussion groups in specific schools with large student groups (30–40 in each group).
- Smaller discussion sessions in schools with 10–20 students in each group.

In total, we conducted 3 large workshops, 10 large discussion groups and 10 smaller discussion sessions. In total, around 1000 young people were spoken to in this phase of the work. The majority of young people spoken to were drawn from secondary schools, with an approximate 70%/30% split between secondary and primary schools.

Data was collected in different ways—large workshops were attended by teams of facilitators who each worked with a small group (approximately 10 young people per group) who made notes during their discussions, as well as providing young people with opportunities to post up their own thoughts and comments with post it notes and flip charts. School-specific discussion groups were generally attended by two or three staff from the digital Headstart team, and a similar approach was used. For the smaller discussions, two researchers attended and discussions were recorded (with the students consent) and audio tracks were analysed. With the whole data set, a thematic analysis was conducted to draw out common themes and discuss "highlights". It was both reassuring and encouraging to note that there was a considerable amount of saturation of themes across the groups and, while activity online, unsurprisingly, differed depending on the age of the students with whom we were speaking. For example, unsurprisingly, adult themes such as pornography did not occur in primary discussions. However, there were plenty of discussions with those students with things like age appropriate games and social media. We are also mindful to record activities young people discussed at different ages, to start to map out what they viewed as "normal" within different age groups.

We did generally keep questions very open ended in discussions to allow these views to be drawn out. Our key foci were:

- What causes upset online?
- Do you worry about how much time you spend online?
- Do you enjoy learning about online safety in school?
- How do you ask for help?
- What can adults do to help?

One theme that often occurred, unsurprisingly, was that adults did not seem to have a strong appreciation of young people's online lives, and often overreacted or accused them of behaving in a manner which a lot of them did not recognise. For example, one young person from a year 10 group (aged 14–15) said that they felt there were lots of stereotypes about young people online that do not play out in reality. They acknowledged that some of their peers would engage in risk behaviour online (such as sending images or meeting up with online "friends"), most were aware of the risks and did not do so. They also said that they felt a lot of adults exaggerate about both the risks online and also young people's behaviours. Adults, they said, always had a story about a young person who ended up dead or seriously harmed as a result of something that happened online.

What Causes Upset Online?

This was generally the opening focus of discussions and resulted in a large amount of feedback that resulted from lived experiences, rather than what they had been told in class. There were a great many different things that came out of these discussions, but one thing that was common was young people talked about upset online arising from people, rather than content. Young people of all ages talked about how upset and abuse might arise in all manner of online situations, but most upset occurred as a result of interaction with others (abuse in gaming, group chats where someone became argumentative, groups "ganging up" or "piling on" on some else, comments on social media meant to upset, late night messages intending to cause conflict, etc.).

While we might generally group this upset in the unhelpful term "cyberbullying" (see below), a more rounded and less emotive term is "peer on peer abuse". We also came across some of the more adultist concerns, such as grooming, and while some were somewhat naïve (e.g. saying they've a friend their age who lives somewhere else, but without being able to provide any evidence that they might be the same age aside from that was what they were told or their profile picture on social media), there was also a great deal of resilience, knowing that there is grooming online (they referred to "pervs" or "pedos"), the fact that this is a message delivered to them a great deal at school (particularly at primary school) and they would generally ignore or block people who made them uncomfortable.

One thing we were mindful of in our discussions was to not confront attendees on their own behaviour, so we would never say "do you do this" or "have you ever done this". Instead, we would use scenarios, media stories or questions like "are you aware of anyone who has ever done this?" to avoid them becoming defensive or feeling challenged. This was generally an effective approach and resulted in much open dialogue about young people online and their thoughts about impact upon wellbeing.

When it came to upsetting content, this was equally wide ranging, and while some would talk about being shown "inappropriate content" (e.g. being shown pornography by a peer), there was also a great deal of discussions around content from those with heavy media presence. Over the duration of this phase of the Headstart project, the Manchester Arena bombing took place, and many young people talked about how it was upsetting to see the news reporting about this as it was about people their age. One other form of upsetting content young people frequently talked about was climate change, which is unsurprising given its prevalence in the media. Again, a lot of the time young people disclosed content that came from mainstream media channels online, rather than specifically online produced content, that was causing upset about climate change.

We did explore gaming considerably, as young people playing "age inappropriate games" is a frequent concern for adults. This concern was generally not shared by young people. There was, again, some evidence of third person effects, with some gamers saying they were resilient to adult content; however, they would not agree with someone younger than them playing a game like that. However, when asked when they started playing "adult" games, they would generally say that they played them when they were younger too!

Most young people felt they, themselves, were resilient to seeing more mature content in games. When asked about adult concerns that playing adult games might cause them to become violent or engaging in risky sexual behaviour, young people we spoke to dismissed this. The biggest harm in games, in their view, was the abuse one might receive via group chats in multi-player games (again highlighting the harm arising from the behaviour of peers, rather than the content of the game), or frustration with the game itself, which might result in "rage quitting", particularly when they were beaten at the last minute in a football game. It was interesting to note that young people viewed sports games, in general, as having great potential for harm because of the competitive nature of them and the capability to abuse while playing. Some disclosed knowledge of fall outs during these sorts of games resulting in physical altercations the following day.

Do You Worry About How Much Time You Spend Online?

The response to this was interesting, given the large amount of concern about young people's screen time. Many young people were very open about the large amount of time they spent online, but were equally open that this was because a great deal of their lives happened online. They were quick to point out that a lot of school work is done online, and this is something that they have to do as part of their education. There were a wide range of other activities that took place online, such as consuming media (Netflix, iPlayer, etc.), interacting with friends, interacting with family, playing games, browsing social media and so on. Most would point out there were very few aspects of their lives that did not have an online element to them. Even when considering something typically "offline" such as sport, they pointed out that there would be arrangements for playing sport that took place online, group chats about the sporting activities, chats about professional sport online and similar.

Some did feel that they spent "too much" time online, but there was little agreement on what "too much" would look like. Some young people who disclosed they spent more than 6 h a day online saw nothing wrong with it, given that every aspect of their lives required some form on online interaction, and others who spent less than an hour were concerned. It was interesting to observe that for some young people whose online consumptions did not seem that great but were concerned were generally told the time was excessive by adults in their lives (parents, teachers, etc.) rather than it being a belief they have developed independently. For example, one young person in year 6 (aged between 10 and 11) said she thought she spent too much time online, but also said she spends less that an hour a day, on average, online. When asked why she thought that was excessive, she said that's what her mother told her.

However, even those who spent a lot of time online but were less concerned were happy to acknowledge Fear Of Missing Out (FOMO) and concerns about online popularity were prevalent. No one wanted to be the first person to leave a group chat so they would sometimes go late into the night, there were concerns caused by seeing friends all together at a party (using things like SnapMaps), and "like anxiety" was also an issue, with jealousy arising if someone else's post was getting more attention that theirs or someone was perceived to be more popular online because they had more friends, or more attention. Some would describe spending long periods of time passively looking at Instagram pages of others but not interacting, which they acknowledged was problematic. So perhaps the responses to this question helped us understand that the concern was less about *the duration* of being online, but *why* they were online and whether they felt pressured to do so.

Do You Enjoy Learning About Online Safety in School?

In general, there was a sympathetic, but negative, response to this question. While comments like "its boring", "we do the same things all of the time" and "we just get shown videos" were common, equally there was a general view that it was clear that a lot of their teachers were not particularly aware of the issues they were supposed to be teaching. One of two things frequently occurred—either students would lose interest quickly or, if the member of staff turned the lesson around and ask their views on aspects of online safety, there was a more positive response.

In general, it was interesting to note that online safety was generally delivered as a short-dedicated session (e.g. a video shown in assembly) or with a "collapsed timetable" day with external speakers. There was little mention of online safety being discussed in a different subject (e.g. in an English class) or consistency of delivery across a prolonged period of weeks. There was a greater likelihood to have an "online safety" session delivered as part of these off timetable weeks where regular lessons were not delivered and instead the young people who take part in classes delivered by, generally, external speakers on a range of social issues, such as drug awareness, sex and relationships, and online safety.

The use of external speakers was an interest thing to get the young people to reflect upon—many saw the benefits of having an "expert" to speak to, so they could ask more risqué questions without risk of a telling off. They also said, however, that one of the issues they face is that they want to have people in their school they can ask questions to on a more ad hoc basis, rather than solely in a twice a year classroom session, and this was not possible if the "experts" were not available outside of these sessions.

How Do You Ask for Help?

It was fair to say that there was not a great deal of faith in adults who have responsibilities for their safeguarding. Young people would say that perhaps there would be one or two staff would be trusted not to "lose it" the general view was they'd get into trouble if they disclosed anything about an online incident. As already discussed in Chapter 3, a lot of young people felt there was no point in disclosing upset or harm to an adult because it was not worth the hassle or the telling off they would receive.

Those they were more likely to disclose to are those staff with the closest pastoral relationship with the young people such as teaching assistants and, to a lesser extent, a class teacher. Senior staff were viewed more as disciplinarians and as such were unlikely to be turned to for a pastoral issue—they were, after all, the staff more like to give the "scary" assembly where they would point out all the scary and dangerous things that happen online. The likelihood of speaking to parents was highly variable, some young people were very happy to do so, some said they would be scared to in case they were told off and a key finding was as they got older the likelihood of disclosing to a parent would reduce, particularly for a more mature issue such as pornography or sexting.

When asking about the tools that were available online to help with dealing with abuse or unwanted contact, again there was a mixed view. Some would actively use reporting mechanisms on games and social media platforms (sometimes to get people "banned" for mischievous or malicious reasons); there was variable view of how useful this was. In a lot of games, they could see responsive platforms where bans and blocks were used well. Few would block people in social media (sometimes it was acknowledged this was down to FOMO—even if someone was being abusive or argumentative it was better to see what they were saying "to your face" rather than "behind your back" and many believed there was no point in reporting people because nothing would be done. A few gave examples of when they had reported upsetting content (generally this was content related to animal abuse) and it was not taken down. Therefore, they said, they knew there was no point in reporting. However, it was encouraging to note many were aware of reporting and blocking routes on both platforms and devices and used them in some circumstance.

WHAT CAN ADULTS TO DO HELP?

A common thread in responses over the whole project (and this has already been talked about in Chapter 2) is these three requests:

- Listen
- Understand
- Don't Judge

As we have discussed before, this is not something that has changed. The "don't judge" call came loud and clear from many young people in our discussions. When a young person turns to an adult for help, as a result of concern or upset about something that might have happened online, or even if they are simply curious about something related to technology and they have a question, it comes as no surprise that they wish to be listened to by someone who can appreciate what has happened and has clear advice on what to do. Or just to answer their question without fear of being told off for asking it. As discussed above, some young people were confident they could do this with *some* adults, and others were less confident. And there was a clear feeling that for some of the more complex issues older teens faced (such as sexting), adults would generally not respond in a calm and supportive manner. It should be noted that it was not just professionals who were viewed like this. When speaking young people from older classes, they were equally concerned about disclosing to a parent. In the case of non-consensual sharing, one young person said they would never be able to disclose that to their parents if it happened to them because their father would "kill" whomever did the sharing.

PARTICULAR ISSUES ARISING

As well as key themes, a lot of issues arose that helped us shape the aspects that would go into the tool, and this is developed further in the following chapter. While some were expected, others were more of a surprise for us:

Cyberbullying—was a term used a great deal for all manner of online abuse from peers and strangers. However, what was less clear was young people's understanding of the term, or what differentiates between someone being mean to someone else online, and what was cyberbullying. An early decision we made in the development of the tool was to avoid the term, because it has because so opaque and broadly used it have become virtually meaningless. Cyberbullying was used to describe activities as diverse as a stranger calling someone a name on a game to persistent long-term online abuse by a peer. What was clear from these discussions is the unhelpfulness of the term and how we needed to be more specific in our descriptions of activities, such as online pile ones, peer on peer abuse, sharing images, etc.

Deep/dark web—Probably one of the most interesting, and confusing, topics of debate related to the use of dark web/deep web technologies. This relates to areas of the internet that are not indexed, and cannot be searched or monitored, as a result of the encryption technologies used (e.g. browsing the web using a Tor browser). The most notorious aspects of deep web technologies (the *dark* web) relate to criminal online activities, such as drug dealing, buying illegal products or accessing illegal content such as child sexual abuse material. However, there are also other *deep* web activities, such as covert browsing, which are innocuous but might be used to circumvent censorious regimes or excessive internet access monitoring. Most "knowledge" on the dark web was somewhat folklore-ish—many talked about it but no one used it and there was a lot of unease in talking about it initially. When this was explored, it was because many young people had been told by staff that the dark web was full of paedophiles, gun sellers and drug dealers and if you go there you will be arrested.

Young people would sometimes mention that they knew someone who had been on the dark web, like this was an edgy and rebellious thing to do. Yet no one we spoke to at this stage had experienced it themselves (this is similar to our broader online safeguarding work—many people have very clear views on the dangers of using deep web technologies, yet have never used them and do not know anyone who does), which does lead us to wonder where the opinions formed about these technologies came from—we discovered this was a mix of peer myths and questioning by concerned adults. Conversely, in our work with professionals during the Headstart project, including professionals who were part of the project, there was clear consensus that the dark web was illegal, harmful and an immediate safeguarding "red flag".

Pornography—The perennial topic of anxiety for adults, young people seemed far more comfortable talking about it when they get the opportunity to! There was general agreement that from year 8 onwards that pornography is part of young people's experiences, and a very normal part by Key Stage 4 (aged between 14 and 16). While there was some gender difference (males were far more likely to access pornography than females), there was generally a view that this happens and we should be talking about it. There were more interesting discussions about people "excessively" using pornography, which generally related to watching in break times or consumption that impacted on other social aspects, such as interacting with friends. There was clearly a view that some of their peers watched too much. However, when asked what we might do to support young people accessing pornography, or concerns they might have about peers doing so, there were few calls to block it or to control access. In general, the discussions we had around pornography, which were with those in Key Stage 4 (between then ages of 14 and 16) there were great calls for education around the topic, because, in the view of most young people, it was impossible to ignore or avoid. Even if young people did not wish to access it themselves, they would receive videos and images in group chats, some from "mainstream" pornography, some intimate images from peers.

The Lure of Online Celebrity—for a lot of younger children the desire to not just be *famous*, but being *online famous*, was something discussed a great deal. In the era of the online influencer, many young people talked about their favourite online celebrities and a wish to have a lifestyle like them—in general it was viewed as both a good way to make money and also having huge amounts of followers would be indicative of success. Deeper conversations (e.g., "how do you think they maintain their popularity?", "what happens when they start to lose subscribers?", "how often do they have to produce new contact and interact with followers?") allowed young people to think more critically about what being an internet celebrity might be like, and it was clear these were not conversations they had been engaged with before.

The Law—There were three very specific things that came out from discussions on what is illegal—young people, in general, were of the view that access pornography, sending nudes/sexting and using social media under the age of 13 were all illegal. They generally believed this because that's what they had been told by adults. It was clear that messages of illegality (alongside the subsequent "you could get arrested for doing that") were frequently used in school settings and discussions with other adults. However, what was equally clear was the way in which these messages were delivered were blunt and imprecise. For each one of these, there are complexities that do not make legality as black and white as they might first seem, and this was something we were mindful to incorporate into the tool.

Fake accounts/catfishing—the use of fake accounts, creating accounts to look like someone else or accounts to defraud (i.e. claiming to be someone else to befriend people online) were all more common than we had expected, and knowledge of them was prevalent.

The Mundane—One final issue that frequently arose in our discussions which, on the face of it, might not seem as significant as other "named" issues and one which we will refer to as "the mundane". These were not specific harms, more the nagging irritation of people getting more likes for a picture or a post than someone else, or the frustration with someone maintaining a SnapChat streak with one friend more than someone else. Issues of popularity, or what makes a good online friend, arose again and again. There was a lot of discussion about how this was the sort of thing that troubled young people on a regular, even daily, basis. They wanted to know how to deal with it but if they raised these issues with adults, they were told to "stop being so silly" or "what are you worried about that for". What was clear that there was little opportunity to discuss these issues in school settings.

CONCLUSIONS

In this chapter, we have explored the research foundations that led to the development of the Online Resilience Tool. This was the first research phase of the tool's development—drawing upon this body of knowledge we drafted a pilot version of the tool and then further engaged with young people for refinement. The following chapter describes that process.

REFERENCES

Brown, C., & Czerniewicz, L. (2010). Debunking the 'digital native': Beyond digital apartheid, towards digital democracy. *Journal of Computer Assisted Learning, 26*(5), 357–369.

Chafouleas, S. M., Johnson, A. H., Overstreet, S., & Santos, N. M. (2016). Toward a blueprint for trauma-informed service delivery in schools. *School Mental Health, 8*(1), 144–162.

Cohen, S. (2011). *Folk devils and moral panics*. Routledge.

Felitti, V. J., Anda, R. F., Nordenberg, D., Williamson, D. F., Spitz, A. M., Edwards, V., & Marks, J. S. (1998). Relationship of childhood abuse and household dysfunction to many of the leading causes of death in adults: The Adverse Childhood Experiences (ACE) Study. *American Journal of Preventive Medicine, 14*(4), 245–258.

GambleAware. (2019). *The effect of gambling marketing and advertising on children, young people and vulnerable adults*. https://about.gambleaware. org/media/1965/17-067097-01-gambleaware_interim-synthesis-report_090 719_final.pdf. Accessed August 2021.

Helsper, E. J., & Eynon, R. (2010). Digital natives: Where is the evidence? *British Educational Research Journal, 36*(3), 503–520.

Kalmakis, K. A., & Chandler, G. E. (2015). Health consequences of adverse childhood experiences: A systematic review. *Journal of the American Association of Nurse Practitioners, 27*(8), 457–465.

Livingstone, S., Davidson, J., & Bryce, J. (2017). *Children's online activities, risks and safety. A literature review by the UKCCIS Evidence Group*. https:// assets.publishing.service.gov.uk/government/uploads/system/uploads/att achment_data/file/759005/Literature_Review_Final_October_2017.pdf. Accessed August 2017.

Mueller, M. (2019). *Challenging the social media moral panic: Preserving free expression under hypertransparency.* Cato Institute. https://www.cato.org/publications/policy-analysis/challenging-social-media-moral-panic-preserving-free-expression-under. Accessed August 2021.

Orben, A., & Przybylski, A. K. (2019). Screens, teens, and psychological well-being: Evidence from three time-use-diary studies. *Psychological Science, 30*(5), 682–696. https://doi.org/10.1177/0956797619830329

Pachter, L. M., Lieberman, L., Bloom, S. L., & Fein, J. A. (2017). Developing a community-wide initiative to address childhood adversity and toxic stress: A case study of the Philadelphia ACE task force. *Academic Pediatrics, 17*(7), S130–S135.

Phippen, A., & Bond, E. (2020). *Organisational responses to social media storms: An applied analysis of modern challenges.* Springer Nature.

Prensky, M. (2001). Digital natives, digital immigrants part 2: Do they really think differently?. *On the horizon.*

Royal College of Psychiatrists. (2020). *Technology use and the mental health of children and young people.* https://www.rcpsych.ac.uk/improving-care/campaigning-for-better-mental-health-policy/college-reports/2020-college-reports/Technology-use-and-the-mental-health-of-children-and-young-people-cr225. Accessed August 2021.

Walkley, M., & Cox, T. L. (2013). Building trauma-informed schools and communities. *Children & Schools, 35*(2), 123–126.

World Health Organisation. (2019). *To grow up healthy, children need to sit less and play more.* https://www.who.int/news-room/detail/24-04-2019-to-grow-up-healthy-children-need-to-sit-less-and-play-more. Accessed August 2021.

CHAPTER 5

Bridging the Divide

Abstract The verification of the Online Resilience Tool, which aimed to provide professionals with a resource to help inform safeguarding responses to disclosed concerns or harms by young people as a result of digitally facilitated behaviours, was conducted through focus group activity with young people and parents of the very young, to determine the placement of behaviours (harmful, potential harmful, not harmful). This research demonstrated that even after development phase underpinned with youth voice, further verification with young people challenged the placement of many behaviours, particularly around more contentious issues such as the dark web.

Keywords Online safety · Digital resilience · Online safety resources · Online harms · Dark web

This chapter will explore the development of the digital resilience tool as a means to provide professionals with a resource to guide rational decision making around online safeguarding.

It will describe how we decided upon the structure of the tool, how the initial behaviours were identified and placed, and how these behaviours evolved through the consultations we held with young people and professionals.

© The Author(s), under exclusive license to Springer Nature   65
Switzerland AG 2022
A. Phippen and L. Street, *Online Resilience and Wellbeing in Young People*, Palgrave Studies in Cyberpsychology,
https://doi.org/10.1007/978-3-030-88634-9_5

It will then look in detail at how young people's views differed from those of the professionals, and how we took these differences into consideration when deciding how to re-classify behaviours.

This chapter will conclude by reflecting on how these different views on risk affect the conversations between young people and professionals about the online world.

Early Development of the Online Resilience Tool

As outlined in Chapter 3, the attitudes, values and beliefs of professionals have historically been more of an influence on their safeguarding decision making around young people's online behaviour than the reality of the risk experienced by young people. It therefore became apparent that a simple and clear safeguarding tool was needed to show whether behaviours constituted a safeguarding concern, or whether they reflected normal exploration of the online world.

To best support professionals in their practice, we decided to split the behaviours into Harmful (meaning an intervention is needed), Potentially Harmful (meaning a conversation must be had to identify if the behaviour is harmful or not) and Not Harmful (meaning no intervention is needed, but positive reinforcement and education should continue). We also split the behaviours into 5 age groups: 0–5 years, 6–8 years, 9–12 years, 13–15 years and 16–18 years.

The older age groups were chosen to reflect the changes in the way young people are viewed by the legal system: A child under 13 can never give consent to a sexual act, between 13 and 16 consent is considered in decision making around safeguarding, and at 16 young people have reached the age of consent and can leave school but are not classed as adults until they turn 18 (Sexual Offences Act, 2003). The younger age groups broadly reflect key stages.

The research phase of the work, described in Chapter 4, highlighted the need for the tool and how best professionals (and later parents/carers) could be upskilled to support young people. They also provided the detail of what young people do online which populated the first draft of the tool, along with the input from the team of professionals developing the tool.

This draft had 129 behaviours listed across the 5 age groups which would evolve into 155 behaviours through focus groups with young people and input from safeguarding professionals.

Focus Groups

The focus groups were arranged through parent toddler groups, schools, colleges and youth clubs in Cornwall. Young people were shown the draft of the tool and asked whether they thought the behaviours were in the correct category (Harmful, Potentially Harmful or Not Harmful), and whether there were any other online activities that should be added. We saw the young people in the same age groups as the tool used (outlined above). For the youngest age group (0–5 years), we spoke to parents.

We ran 11 focus groups with the age breakdown as follows:

Parents of 0–5 age group—10 parents
6–8 age group—6 children
9–12 age group—4 children
13–15 age group—16 young people
16–18 age group—46 young people

We had a disproportionate number for each group due to the different amounts of time schools, colleges and youth groups were able to give us. We opted to speak to parents of the youngest age group because they act as gatekeepers to their child's online activity.

All focus groups had another adult present, whether a teacher or youth worker from the youth group.

For children in the 6–8 and 9–12 age groups, we amended some of the language used to ensure they would understand the behaviour and would not be upset by it. For example, we changed "games with fantasy violence" to "games with cartoons who fight each other" and "accessing pornography" to "accessing grown-up content on purpose".

We ran focus groups as informal group discussions, and participants were also given paper to record any other thoughts they did not wish to share with the whole group. We opted for discussions rather than surveys because, although we may have been able to get a higher number of responses with a survey, it was important to understand the young people's motivation for their feedback, which was only possible through this qualitative approach (Bagnoli & Clark, 2010). We wanted to ensure we weren't simply asking young people to parrot the online safety messages they had received through their education, and using a questionnaire may have forced the young people to relay these messages, providing them with answers they would be unlikely to express otherwise (Nicholas, 2000). The focus groups allowed us to delve into young people's actual experience and identify when lack of personal experience led them to fall back on these online safety messages.

The focus groups also enabled us to gently question these safety messages to see whether the children and young people thought they were useful and used by children their age. This helped us to identify ambivalence in the young people through their non-verbal communication (Nicholas, 2000).

One of the problems we experienced with running these focus groups was that often one or two young people would lead the whole group (Smithson, 2000). This led to whole groups of young people stating the same belief because one or two dominant young people suggested it.

We did expect this to happen and took a few measures to overcome it. The first was to arrange focus groups with groups of young people who would not necessarily be confident to get their voice heard in a larger, heterogenous group. We asked a Special School and an LGBT support group if we could meet with their young people, as well as asking schools to arrange focus groups with specific cohorts of young people.

Unfortunately, the special school did not respond to our requests. And, as ethnic diversity in Cornish schools is quite low, the schools which were able to support the focus groups were not able to provide a separate group of young people of a similar age from BAME backgrounds. We did meet with 2 groups of LGBT young people which allowed us to ensure this groups' voice was present in the tool.

Another measure we took was to split large groups into 2 smaller groups; this better enabled us to record the depth of the conversation while minimising the impact of one dominant young person.

However, even with these measures, there were a number of groups who had one or two very vocal young people whose opinions influenced the whole group.

Another issue was that the focus groups had to be run as a cross between an education session, a youth group and a research group. The reasons for this were as follows:

- Education session—young people did not always have experience of the behaviour we were talking about, or had no experience of adults talking to them about it. Therefore, in order to ensure we were talking about the same issue, we had to first explain what it was.

- Youth group—as youth workers it was natural for us to take a youth work approach to these groups, including having a "group agreement" and actively engaging the young people, rather than simply asking questions and awaiting responses.
- Research group—bring our alternative persona as researchers, we did have specific questions we wanted to ask the young people, so when conversation veered too far from the topic, we would ask specific questions to bring it back.

This approach made the setting quite informal, and therefore, sometimes teachers or youth workers would ask leading rather than open questions and would guide the discussion in an effort to be helpful. Equally, young people would sometimes ask us our opinions on issues, and our answers would inevitably guide the discussion.

The beauty of this informal approach was that it allowed us to have interesting and varied discussions with the young people based on their interest and knowledge of the issues. For example, with a group of 13- to 15-year-old boys, we had a long discussion about what they enjoyed about online gaming, which illuminated a great deal of activities linked to gaming which we had not anticipated. Equally, a group of 16- to 18-year-old young women spoke at length about their views and concerns about young men their age watching porn, covering their frustrations over what these young men expected women's bodies to look like, to fears that it would have a long-term negative impact on the young men's ability to have healthy, happy sex lives in the future.

EMERGING ISSUES FROM FOCUS GROUPS

There were some areas which generated a lot of interesting discussion, and these are explored below. When we reflect upon these findings, we see some similarities with the initial discussions with young people which convinced us of the need for the tool and allowed us to shape the early draft. It also allowed us to be confident that we had reached a point of saturation when exploring some of the key issues around online safeguarding, young people's use of digital technology and its impact upon their wellbeing. However, it also further improved our appreciation of the complexities of young people's use of digital technology and the importance of an individual response to young people's disclosures of online harm—different activities clearly impact on young people depending on their existing knowledge, resilience, support structures and personality. We cannot simply say that behaviour x requires response y. It became clear that the most significant part of the tool would be the "potentially harmful" category, where we were essentially guiding the professional to discover more from the disclosure to consider appropriate response.

The Dark Web

In many discussions with the 13–15 and 16–18 age groups, young people said accessing the dark web should be in Harmful. They had a very limited understanding of the deep web and mostly had no understanding of the difference between the deep web and the dark web. Many felt, quite strongly, that anyone accessing it could only be doing so for nefarious purposes.

> ...I would change one of the amber ones to red – accessing dark web.
>   Young person, 16–18 age group

> Dark web should be in red as it's dangerous. (emphasis in original)
>   Young person, 16–18 age group

These responses helped us identify that we needed to be clearer about the distinction between the deep web and the dark, specifically splitting them to show that accessing the "dark web" refers to accessing illegal content and accessing the deep web is just using a browser such as TOR to mask their identity; we also included these definitions in the glossary of the tool as we realised that professionals would likely also need this clarification (Headstart Kernow, 2020).

In the majority of our discussions with young people, even after being given this distinction, they did not feel that there was any legitimate reason to access the deep web.

That is, until we spoke to an LGBT group. In this group, the understanding of the dark web was far more nuanced. It was the first group we spoke to where the young people admitted to having accessed the deep web. Their reasons for using it were usually around exploring their sexuality or gender identity without any risk of being "outed" before they were ready.

Talking to this group of young people revealed a vulnerability while also highlighting an important function of this online behaviour. The vulnerability was that a young person who is exploring their sexuality or gender identity on the deep web would be at high risk of being groomed, harassed or receiving unsolicited sexual advances. Being young, likely not yet "out", and inexperienced in relationships generally would mean they would be less able to identify risks, and may be less likely to seek help if something went wrong for fear of outing themselves. If they lived in a household where homophobia, biphobia or transphobia were present, they would be even less likely to seek help, especially as this may be why they were using the deep web in the first place.

This high level of risk for this clearly very vulnerable group of young people would surely make any professional want to start safeguarding procedures. However, the function of the behaviour should also be recognised. The young person may need to explore their identity in order to be able to talk about it. Many parents may not know or understand the terms pansexual or asexual. They may be opposed to transgender issues, or be confused by the idea of non-binary people. Therefore, they might not discuss these issues with their children, or if they do, might (deliberately or inadvertently) state homophobic or transphobic views. While these identities may be becoming more mainstream as whole, a non-binary 15-year-old will need to learn what non-binary means before they are able to come out as such.

After many deep discussions with young people and with the other professionals involved in the development of the tool, we decided that this behaviour should be categorised as Potentially Harmful. If a young person says they've accessed the deep web to explore their sexuality, and they are now ready to come out as pansexual, we shouldn't be starting safeguarding procedures because they've accessed the deep web, but instead talking to them about how we can best support them. That discussion should rightly cover whether they had any bad experiences while on the deep web, which may well require a safeguarding referral, but it should also cover what support or social groups for LGBTQIA+ young people they can access, where they can find reliable information about these issues and who they can go to for help with any more research they might want to do.

This is a perfect example of the importance of finding out more when a Potentially Harmful behaviour is identified.

Sending/Receiving Nudes

Another hotly debated behaviour was that of nudes. Firstly, it caused a great deal of disagreement among the young people, and later a similar amount among the professionals. Some of the issues are identified and explored below.

1. It's illegal, so don't do it.

Most young people have heard this message. They know it's illegal. Actually, I was surprised about the level of knowledge they had about the law. They knew that it was illegal for them to take nudes of themselves, for them to send them to other people and for other people to look at and/or keep those messages.

The youngest age group that we talked about nudes to was 9–12; this was because for younger age groups we had not included sending nudes/sexting in the first draft of the tool. For 9- to 12-year-olds, sending nudes/sexting is categorised as a Harmful behaviour, and certainly, at this age, we would expect to see a safeguarding response if young people were found to be engaging in this behaviour. The children in the focus groups agreed that this was the correct place, but interestingly they also felt that adults could best support them by helping them remove any naked pictures of them. Sadly, in talking to professionals about online safeguarding, even though they know the distribution of these images is illegal, many do not know the mechanism for removal.

2. Sharenting

For the 9–12 age group, one issue that caused much discussion was the fact that their parents had naked baby photos of them on their Facebook page. These pictures had existed for years on this page, but the young people had reached an age when their peers might seek out these images in order to embarrass and humiliate one another. All the children we spoke to, from 6 years old upwards, didn't like their parents having so many pictures of them online, but the fact that these photos could then be shared around a friendship group or class as a method of bullying was of particular concern. While these images wouldn't be considered illegal to the letter of the law, as they were not intended to be indecent (Crown Prosecution Service, 2018) the children and young people in these focus groups did make that distinction—naked photos of themselves that were shared around their consent were humiliating regardless of the nature of the photos.

3. "Accidental" Nudes

In the 13- to 15-year-old age group, one interesting discussion with a group of boys was around images being sent to them without their consent. This was not about the unsolicited "dick pic" but rather that if pictures are doing the rounds, they felt it would be very unfair if they were punished for receiving it if they had never asked for it in the first place. Discussions on this subject also touched on the idea that young people would delete these images straight away but some messaging services (such as WhatsApp) would save them without the young people necessarily knowing, again meaning they may be in possession of an illegal image without their knowledge. This also raised concerns about how to report these images. If a young person was sent an illegal image without their consent, should they delete it completely, or keep it in order to report it? The message of "it's illegal, don't do it" has so muddied the water that young people do not know how to help keep other young people safe.

Interestingly, in the 16–18 age group, the discussion of "accidentally" receiving nudes was viewed with much hilarity, especially by one group of young women, who felt that anyone claiming to have "accidentally" received a nude was probably lying to get themselves out of trouble with whoever had found it.

There was a great deal of cynicism from the young women in this particular group; their attitude towards young men their age was that boys their age were less mature than them and were always just out for whatever they could get, whether it was nudes or a physical sexual relationship. The young women saw themselves as the gatekeepers of this, with some expressing the idea that if you send a nude you should expect it to get shared around all the boys. Young men seemed less aware of this, and none of them said they would share an image with others if it was sent to them, whether this was a case of only sharing views that would be well received by the group (Smithson, 2000) was not clear from the discussions.

4. Intimidation

In one of the focus groups with 16- to 18-year-olds, there was a concern that some of their peers may be using sexual images to intimidate other people, whether a selfie or something sourced online. The young women seemed particularly concerned about being sent these images. They were able to talk eloquently about the issues they had dealing with these situations as they felt the young men sending them were likely to react badly if they asked them to stop, and that it might result in even more intimidating images being sent. Many young women expressed the view that the only way of dealing with this behaviour was to ignore it. This was therefore not something they would be likely to report and they did not feel parents/carers or professionals in their lives would be able to help them even if they did report it.

It was interesting that this was noted as the converse situation (where young women send nudes to males) was not something they were able to use to the same effect. Males in their lives could intimidate them by sending images, and by receiving them, suggesting a highly gendered experience of sharing these images.

Young men we spoke to did not see the sending of images as intimidating, but were not able to articulate why they might send an image.

Social Media

Many of the young people we spoke to had had bad experiences as a result of social media. These were not experiences of grooming or "catfishing" (receiving messages from someone pretending to be someone else). In fact, in the focus groups, there was not even in-depth discussion of bullying through social media. The main concern that young people had around social media was the anxiety it caused them.

One element of this was "fear of missing out" (FOMO) (described as "the mundane" in Chapter 4), where young people felt they had to perform on social media so as to prove they were having a really good time—and even though they knew that what they posted wasn't an accurate representation of what they experienced, they still felt envious when seeing how much fun other people were having.

Another element was around body image. Young men in the 13–15 age group said that they knew friends (generally girls) who always used apps like "face tune" to enhance their appearance, which they thought was a bad thing as it would make people feel bad about themselves.

This group of young men also thought that although compulsive social media use was definitely a bad thing, it was pretty normal.

All the young people we spoke to between 13 and 18 years old said that although they thought looking at your phone at night was probably not good, they didn't think it was a big problem, as long as you just checked messages and then went back to sleep. Some people identified that sitting up all night scrolling would be bad, but on the whole, young people didn't feel that looking at a device at or after bedtime was a problem.

Gaming

There were a variety of thoughts around gaming. Parents of the youngest age group felt that children in the 0–5 age group should not be exposed to any age-restricted games, with many parents stating that they did not even use devices around their children (although it was not clear whether this included Smart TVs and streaming services). Children in the 5–7 and 8–12 focus groups actually tended to agree with parents, saying that games with violence should be in the Harmful category. One young person expressed this by saying about games and violent TV shows and films:

> When you get stressed it stops you being a child.
>   Child, 8–12 age group

For those over 13, the issue of age-restricted gaming was more relaxed. There was a general sense that if someone is playing age-restricted games and their parents have agreed to it, it's probably fine, with the caveat from one group that parents should make sure they know what the game is about so they can make an informed decision.

One group of young men in the 13–15 age group said that although Fortnite is a 12 (PEGI rating), there were loads of younger kids playing it. This was described as quite unpleasant for these young men as they didn't want to get screamed at by a load of kids.

With regard to the risk of grooming and catfishing in these games, they said that if you are aware of it happening, it ruins the game. This was not to say they would rather not know, but with games where they were working collaboratively with other people, leaving a group may mean having to start from scratch with minimal strength and abilities—which would be a huge disappointment after months of building those things up. They said they would probably just stop playing in that case, rather than starting again.

The same group of young men said that their parents were much stricter about them staying up at night playing on game consoles than about playing on their phones. In some cases, this meant they could keep playing even after they had been told to turn off the console as some games are also accessible on a phone. However, in the main, the sense was that this was unfair, with siblings being allowed to scroll through social media long after the young men had been told to stop playing.

Recognising the Behaviours

We also asked young people whether they thought parents/carers or teachers would recognise any of the Harmful behaviours, and whether they would recognise them in their friends. The majority of those who responded said that it might be obvious that something was wrong, but really the only way to know would be if the person told you.

One respondent also said in relation to whether a parent/carer or teacher would know what to do if you told them one of the Harmful behaviours was happening to you that their lack of knowledge might result in them thinking the young person disclosing was joking.

Overwhelmingly, the sense from young people was that adults would not recognise when something was wrong, and that even if they did (or were told) they would still not know what to do about it.

Making the Changes to the Tool

Once all the focus groups had been run, we collated all the feedback and went through each point to assess whether to make the proposed change or not. We considered the number of young people who had made the suggestion and whether there were other safeguarding concerns around the changes. We rejected 37 suggestions and accepted 50, some of which were amended.

Some of the suggestions were rejected because they were too specific, such as creating memes, parties on snap chat and accessing Omegle. These were covered by more general behaviours such as "making content and publishing online', and 'online interaction with strangers". Others were rejected because they do not reflect the best way to protect young people, for example "move phone after bedtime to green" and "move taking a selfie to red". The latter was from a young woman who said that for her, taking a selfie was a sign of poor mental health. She had struggled with eating disorders and body dysmorphia, so if someone saw her taking a selfie, it would be a sign that she was on a downward spiral and would need some support. This showed incredible insight from the young person into her own digital life, and should be applauded. For the majority of young people, this would not be the case but it does serve to highlight the fact that young people are often able to articulate the risk they face in greater depth with better understanding than professionals may give them credit for.

Of the suggestions we did accept, we added 26 behaviours, amended the wording of 22 behaviours and moved 6 behaviours. For example, "sending/receiving nudes" was placed in Harmful for 9- to 12-year-olds and Potentially Harmful for 13- to 15-year-olds. Young people suggested adding "pressuring someone to send nudes" and "selling nudes". The published version of the tool now has 8 distinct behaviours relating to the sending and receiving of nudes which are included in age groups from 6 to 18 years.

The purpose of consulting with young people wasn't simply to tick a box, or to assume that they knew more about staying safe online than we did. In fact, a point that we always come back to when talking to professionals about Online Resilience is that as professionals we know a lot more about managing risk than young people. During adolescence, young people are predisposed to want to take risks and explore their identity (Harris, 2013). The internet simply provides them with a new environment in which to do this. As discussed in Chapter 2, the "digital natives" narrative is frequently brought to bear but rejected—young people don't have an innate understanding of the risks they may be facing online.

Conclusion

Through the focus groups and discussion with professionals working with young people, we found a disparity between perceived problems and threats online. Some of these were driven by young people wanting to engage in certain behaviours which we could not, in good conscience, say were healthy—for example looking at their social media at night.

Others were a result of professionals having a poor grasp of what young people actually do online, which prevents them being able to have meaningful discussions with young people about their online lives.

Our aim was to close this gap by outlining the specific behaviour professionals should be looking for, rather than looking at the app/game/platform.

By consulting with young people, we were able to ensure the behaviours listed in the tool reflected the wide-variety of activities young people engaged in online, and by sharing this with colleagues across the sector, we were able to phrase this in a way professionals would accept and understand.

While not all suggested changes were applied to the final version of the tool, we considered every suggestion on its individual merits and added or amended 50 behaviours.

In the next chapter, we will discuss how the tool was received by professionals in the field generally, as well as the issues created by professionals' own expectations and values.

References

Bagnoli, A., & Clark, A. (2010). Focus groups with young people: A participatory approach to research planning. *Journal of Youth Studies, 13*(1), 101–119. https://doi.org/10.1080/13676260903173504

Crown Prosecution Service. (2018). *Indecent and prohibited images of children.* CPS. https://www.cps.gov.uk/legal-guidance/indecent-and-prohibited-images-children. Accessed August 2021.

Harris, P. (2013). *Youthoria.* Russel House Publishing.

Headstart Kernow. (2020). *Online Resilience Tool.* Headstart Kernow. https://www.headstartkernow.org.uk/digital-resilience/. Accessed August 2021.

Nicholas, D. (2000). *Assessing information needs: Tools, Techniques and concepts for the internet age* (2nd ed.). Taylor & Francis Group.

Sexual Offences Act 2003. (2003). *Sexual Offences Act 2003.* legilsation.gov.uk. https://www.legislation.gov.uk/ukpga/2003/42/contents. Accessed August 2021.

Smithson, J. (2000). Using and analysing focus groups: Limitations and possibilities. *International Journal of Social Research Methodology, 3*(2), 103–119. https://doi.org/10.1080/136455700405172

CHAPTER 6

Embedding and Empowering

Abstract The launch of the Headstart Kernow Online Resilience Tool was accompanied by staff training and an exploration of deployment of the tool among the children's workforce (predominantly in schools). Training further illustrated the variation in knowledge among professionals and adultist perspectives on harm prevention, rather than harm reduction. Findings from the training highlights how deeply rooted a lot of these views were, even if there was little evidence to reinforce them, and how cultural change around online safeguarding must be a long-term goal.

Keywords Online safety · Online harms · Digital resilience · Critical thinking · Evidence based practice

This final research chapter explores the deployment of the tool and its impact. As we have discussed throughout this book, we did not want to simply present the development of a new online safeguarding resource as the end point of a research project. The tool was developed and deployed in June 2020 with complimentary training, which allowed us once more to explore professional's concerns, and better understand knowledge barriers, which informs the knowledge base around online safeguarding.

A. Phippen and L. Street, *Online Resilience and Wellbeing in Young People*, Palgrave Studies in Cyberpsychology,
https://doi.org/10.1007/978-3-030-88634-9_6

As we will discuss throughout this chapter, a key emergent factor in this phase of the research was to see the lack of critical thinking among some professionals—a potentially serious barrier to young people engaging with them which has been a key thread running through this book. Many professionals would voice concerns based upon conjecture and opinion, with no grounding in evidence.

A common example of this is incorrect knowledge of law and its uses to justify prohibitive approaches. To take a perennial favourite, it is illegal for young people under the age of 13 to be on social media. Rather than exploring the factual basis for this conjecture, professionals would use it as an excuse to shut down conversations with young people—they should not be using the platforms, and speaking to them about it will just encourage them. Interactions in training gave the opportunity to both develop the knowledge of professionals and pro-actively challenge these views, encouraging a more open and critical approach to dialogue with young people—supported by the tool as a starting point for whether concern needed to be expressed regarding a disclosed behaviour.

Professional Feedback

However, prior to the exploration of the training proper, it is worthwhile to reflect on an experience that occurred towards the end of the tool's development and launch. We have attempted, throughout this text, to provide the narrative around the development of the Online Resilience Tool and used this as a vehicle to observe the wider challenges in the online safeguarding world. In particular, developing a more effective culture of trust between adults and young people such that there is confidence that disclosure of harm will result in support and rectification, not punishment and judgement. Given the participative nature of the project, we are able to provide vignettes and anecdotes which highlight these challenges and illustrate the barriers we need to overcome.

As discussed in Chapter 5, once we have developed the tool and refined it as a result of young people's feedback (as we have been keen throughout the project to be youth lead and provide authentic youth voice in the work), and as touched upon at the end of the previous chapter, we also sought validation from professionals. Clearly, this is an important part of wishing to engage professionals with a new resource and approach to something that impacts upon their practice. We did not want to appear to have a tool that professionals should just use because we thought it was good, we wanted to work with professionals across the sector to achieve feedback on the tool and gain buy-in with our approach. Given our wide ranging experiences in working across the children's workforce both regionally and nationally, we understood the importance of getting others to champion approaches across their networks.

Once we had made (or rejected) the changes suggested by the young people, we sent the tool to a range of professionals working with young people, including the local lead for Prevent, Designated Safeguarding Leads in youth work organisations and Children's Social Care. These included:

- The Chair of Ethics Committee for a leading child safeguarding charity
- A Safeguarding lead at the DfE
- An independent consultant in RSE
- Headteachers from one primary and one secondary school in Cornwall
- The Prevent Lead for Cornwall
- A director from a leading online safety NGO

Some of the feedback highlighted issues of phrasing, for example "withdrawal issues", was listed as Harmful for the 0–5 age group, but it soon became clear that this was not detailed enough for many professionals to be able to identify in a child—any child may become distressed upon having something taken away from them with no reason given and no other activity to distract them, so on the one hand it could seem to be general, and on the other hand we did not want professionals to only look for the extreme withdrawal that may be associated with drug use. It was later amended to "Upset or aggressive response to withdrawal of device (beyond what is normal for the child)".

Another colleague pointed out that the way we had suggested dealing with issues may have inadvertently suggested not informing children of the law. This was the phrase:

> We should not tell young people that sending nudes is illegal, as we risk re-victimising those who are being abused as a result of taking and sending an image.

This was addressed by adding the word "simply" and it now reads:

> We should not simply tell young people that sending nudes is illegal, as we risk re-victimising those who are being abused as a result of taking and sending an image.

Making these changes was important to show professionals that we had listened and therefore to ensure buy-in from professionals across the county (and the country). We knew there was a risk small issues had the potential to turn whole teams away from using the tool because the language did not sit comfortably with their safeguarding policies.

Professionals did not suggest adding any behaviours to the tool at this stage (nor have they at any point since its deployment). This gives us confidence that the tool has comprehensive coverage of online behaviours faced by young people and recognised by professionals.

We made it clear to all consulted that this was a tool with young voice at its heart and we were guided in the main by the validation from young people. However, it was a worthwhile exercise to consult with external stakeholders to evaluate both tone and value—we were looking for validation rather than another round of editing. Overall, with the exception of a few minor changes and refinements (particularly around screen time where we elaborated on the types of screen time and how passivity was potentially more harmful than active engagement), there were no modification to the tool as a result of this consultation, and the tool was well received. Those in front line delivery could all see that value of the tool and we keen to engage with it, and others came back with offers of promotion across their networks once the tool is finalised.

However, we did face one challenge that illustrated very clearly how poor knowledge and digital value bias can result in exactly the sort of preventative messaging that young people tell us means that they will not disclose harm to adults.

We were intending to work with another NGO on the development and release of the tool. The NGO is a national organisation which focusses in the main on sex and relationships education, and sexual health in general. We saw this as a positive and complimentary relationship, particularly given how young people had frequently told us about the role of digital technology in personal and sexual relationships. However, when we provided the organisation with a draft of the tool, after much delay, their feedback presented a fundamental challenge for the partnership to work.

We were told that, in order to work with them on the project, all mentions of sending intimate images had to be listed as "harmful", regardless of the age of the young person. When challenged on their rationale for this, we were told it's because it's "illegal". Clearly, this was in conflict with young people, who had told us through the project that the issues around legality of exchanging intimate images, and how this is expressed in school settings, are exactly the reason they do not disclose to adults in the event of further non-consensual sharing. We were further told that there were "new laws" that made it clear "sexting was unacceptable", we had to use the term sexting "because that's what young people say" and we would be giving out the wrong message if we said there were some activities that would not be harmful.

Clearly, there are no new laws on the exchange of intimate images among minors in the UK, as we have been told in many discussions with young people that "only people over 40 call it sexting". However, when challenged on this, the view remained that what they were doing was illegal and therefore should be categorised as harmful. This was after we pointed out that many young people had talked about how the exchange of intimate images within a relationship was typical and harm generally occurred when the images were non-consensually shared.

When asked whether they would say that any minor engaged in sexual activity would be harmful, they said this would not be the case (which we are not surprised about given this organisation does a lot of work with minors who become pregnant). Even though the premise was the same (illegal = harmful), they could not see parallels with what they were calling for with digital issues. For some, ultimately undetermined, reason, digital made it different, which highlighted to us once more that even those who claim a progressive voice will bring their own value biases to safeguarding discussions.

And as a result of these discussions, we stopped working with the organisation and continued with the majority of intimate image behaviours (except in younger categories) as "potentially harmful", as we had been told by many young people.

REFLECTIONS FROM OBSERVATIONS WITH THE PROFESSIONAL TRAINING SESSIONS

Moving on to observations from training, as we have described elsewhere in this book, the intention of the project was not just to launch a resource that would be downloaded and used by professionals with no guidance, we intended to provide training for professionals alongside the launch of the tool. Given the launch time of the tool—June 2020—the intention for face-to-face training was abandoned to incorporate online delivery methods that had become so prevalent during the first COVID-19 lockdown. In one way, this was a beneficial outcome—professionals had become used to using online technology for meetings, and we could make sure of pre-sessional online resources and focus the live part of the training on questions and answers and discussion. However, we do acknowledge that some of the value of delivering training face to face is the greater opportunity for group discussion and learning from peers, which was a challenge in online delivery.

The training comprised a number of elements:

- A recorded talk providing an overview of the tool, going through the different types of behaviours and how to respond, and an exploration of the behaviours themselves.
- Some "myth busting" online activities, which allowed professionals to explore their own knowledge of online safeguarding issues (e.g. "legal or illegal?" scenarios which looked at things like accessing the dark web and pornography). These were again delivered in an online package the profession could do on their own. This a useful technique that exploited the asynchronous nature of some of the online training—it allowed professionals to test their knowledge without being put in a situation where they had to demonstrate it in front of others.
- An hour of online "face-to-face" discussion with an expectation that attendees will have done the other online elements prior to attending.

To date, we have had approximately 200 professionals attend the training, which provides us with a useful evidence base to reflect upon its impact and also to observe professionals' wider concerns around online safeguarding. While the training was intended in the first instance to be aimed at education professionals, we soon expanded (due to demand) to other sectors such as youth workers and social care. The majority of attendees did come from education settings; however, a significant minority also came from the wider children's workforce and, as word of mouth spread awareness of the training, more professionals signed up to sessions.

What we present below are observations from the face-to-face aspects of the sessions. While there were few surprises from these sessions, what observations we did collect gave us both confidence about a youth-centric approach for the tool and also how the tool fits into a wider culture change around online safeguarding.

"But It's Illegal"

One thing we were not surprised about, and had reinforced throughout the training, was that legal issues were frequently used within preventative narrative, and professionals were surprised with the pre-sessional material that burst some of these legal perceptions prior to the discussion sessions. While we have already talked, at length, about the legalities around the exchange of intimate images among minors, and this was certainly a strongly held, but poorly understood, view by many professionals, we also observed some other key legal myths, including that it was illegal for a child to play an age inappropriate game, it was illegal for a child to access pornography, and it is illegal for a child to be on social media under the age of thirteen.

This, obviously, reflected what we had been told by young people, and this is no surprise given it would have been professionals similar to those in the training sessions who had delivered this education to the young people. When we expanded upon these legal issues, and highlighted that they are all more complex that preventative "it's illegal, don't do it messages", there was always a lot of surprise. If we take, for example, the perennial favourite of "don't go on social media until you're thirteen", most professionals believed that this was due to safeguarding legislation, rather than the reality of data protection law maintaining that a minor under the age of 13 being unable to consent to their data being collected by a platform (as set out in both the US Children's Online Privacy Protection Act 1998 [Federal Trade Commission, 1998], the EU General Data Protection Regulation 2016 (GDPR) [European Union, 2016] and national implementations of the GDPR, such as the UK's Data Protection Act 2018 [UK Government, 2018]).

Sometimes the challenges to legal assumptions were met with surprise and thanks, sometimes they were met with disappointment. We have observed this is our other work with professionals, sometimes these legal messages are far easier to deliver than more complex supportive messaging. If we say "don't do it, it's illegal", we can immediately project blame onto the victim if they then engage in something, which, of course, harks back to one of the key reasons young people tell us they will not disclose, they do not want to "get judged".

Nevertheless, within these training activities, what was clearly illustrated was the value of moving legal knowledge from preventative to deeper knowledge, as this helps break down the disclosure barrier with young people.

"WELL, MY CHILD/GRANDCHILD WOULD NEVER DO THIS"

One thing that is constant with both the training delivered by headstart and also our wider practice, is that many professionals will bring a parental perspective to online safeguarding training and decision making.

During the training, there have been many times where a professional will start to talk about a conversation about their children, or how they have observed how their child behaves with digital technology, or how "my kids have left home now but I've seen my grandchildren on these devices all of the time". From one perspective, this is to be expected— we bring our own experiences into professional practice all of the time, it is human nature. However, we did often unpick whether this was an appropriate thing to do in a safeguarding judgement, which needs to be evidence led. If we use as the foundation of our judgement "well, my child wouldn't do this", we are, of course, bringing our own value biases to bear in professional judgement. If one's own child would not do something, yet a young person with whom one is working has disclosed it, we immediately bring judgement on them—they've done wrong. While this was discussed at length, and it is frequently acknowledged as problematic by professionals, it happens in virtually every session. It would seem this is a difficult thing to remove from the discourse, but we would at least hope when professionals do revert to parent in their judgements, they are at least cognisant of their actions.

"IT'S THE PARENT'S FAULT"

Developing the parental theme, another recurring discussion as what we might regard as deflection—the view of a professional that regardless of what they do—it will be impossible to resolve an issue because "the parents just let them do it anyway". There are a couple of key facets to this discussion. Firstly, the permissive parent, that will allow their child to have, for example, "a mobile phone far too young" in the (biased) view of the professional, or "buy them inappropriate games". We also hear professionals talking about the lack of awareness of online safeguarding issues and how efforts to education (such as parents online safety sessions in the school) are rarely well attended.

The second facet is the *parental pile on*, generally through social media. Two children will fall out about a digital issue, make complaints to the school and calls for intervention, and while the children resolve their disagreement, the parents are fully engaged on social media criticising both the children and also the school for not dealing with the problem effectively.

We would certainly observe through our wider practice that parents, obviously, have a role to play in the safeguarding of their children and that they can be both supportive and problematic. We have spoken to many young people who say they would not disclose to parents for risk of punishment or judgement, and we have spoken to parents about how they "would not expect this behaviour" from their children. Equally, we have spoken to young people who are confident that they can disclose harms and gain support from their parents, and parents who reflect upon their own behaviour when they were younger, and how their own children are experiencing similar, just on a more public, or digital, stage.

When it comes to parents making use of social media to exacerbate issues, we have every sympathy with professionals and often remind them of their employer's duty of care towards them. While freedom of speech is a perennial claim by online trolls, libel and slander are both things where a professional might expect the support of their employer. Again, there is no easy answer to this, but it does remind us that parents are of course a stakeholder in their children's safety and there should be discourse between stakeholders in this regard.

We have, over the last year, developed a parental offer[1] to compliment the more complex professional's tool. Working with parents groups in the Headstart Kernow group, the general view was that parents are worried about online harms (and who can blame them if their primary source of

---

[1] https://www.headstartkernow.org.uk/digital-resilience/parent-digital-offer/.

information related to children's use of online technologies is the media?) and some sort of "panic reduction" tool would be valuable. As a result of these discussions, we have produced a reduced version of the tool for different age groups that have key behaviours and some general guidance about supporting young people who disclose upset or harm. While it is too early to reflect upon the efficaciousness of these resources for parents, they have been well received by a lot of professionals who see them as a valuable tool to better engage parents and make sure parents and professionals are both approaching online safeguarding from the same perspective.

"Safeguarding Alert – Panic!"

A number of attendees at training talked about the concerns and, in some cases, panic, that resulted from a safeguarding alert being distributed across the local authority. Clearly, again, raising alerts is done for the best on intentions, but something they lack a level of critical thinking before release. Generally from law enforcement, these alerts would spread quickly across a region and will result in senior leaders cascading concerns to safeguarding leads who are told to "do something!". In our discussions around these alerts, the key thing we always return to is "apply some critical thinking to the alert before reacting too strongly".

A perennial favourite is something along the lines of "We've been sent a list of the top ten most dangerous apps and our students use four of them!". Police forces, it seems, are very keen on distributing lists of "dangerous apps" and urge professionals and parents to check whether their young people use them. These lists are generally produced as a result of investigations and national/international police initiatives to explore the sort of platforms used in cases that result in online harms.

The problem is, however, all that these lists do is reflect what is popular among young people. Apps where, for example, grooming occur will be the apps used by children and, sadly, predators with a sexual interest in children will follow. In 2018, a BBC news article raised concerns that Kik Messenger (a now defunct messaging platform similar to WhatsApp and Signal) was used in "over a thousand grooming cases". On the face of it this is cause for concern if young people disclosed using this platform. However, a simple examination of Kik Messenger suggests that it had been downloaded over 300 million times. So, what the headline should have said is "popular messaging platform very rarely used for child abuse". A similar statistic, but one that is less likely to attract much attention might be "1000 predators wear trainers while grooming children". Wearing trainers is not the causation, similarly it is rarely the app that is dangerous, and it is the behaviour upon it, which is why young people need to be confident that if they see something upsetting on a platform, or they are asked to do something they are uncomfortable with, they need to get support and help in removing the content or blocking and reporting an abuser. What they do not need to hear is "its on the dangerous app list, you've only got yourself to blame" or "if you hadn't installed that dangerous app, you wouldn't have been abused".

In one case dealt with within the Headstart Kernow project, we were contacted about a "dangerous game", that would "encourage children to engage with county lines", a emergent form of drug dealing where vulnerable young people were groomed in to acting as distributors in their respective regions (Robinson et al., 2019). Of course this triggered concerns for use, given our previous work trying to debunk the causation between playing video games and acting upon what takes place in video games. With brief investigation, it turned out that the game was very basic app–based game that was generally receiving poor reviews and had been downloaded less than one thousand times. However, one review, clearly sarcastic, said "great for teaching kids about drug dealing". This was all that it took to diffuse the situation and remove the impending safeguarding alert.

Clearly, this is an issue that requires dialogue between stakeholders, but from the training we could see that in a lot of cases professionals needed reassurance not a little critical thinking can deescalate these well-intentioned but potentially harmful concerns very quickly. One only needs to reflect upon the panic around the Momo Challenge (Phippen & Bond, 2019) to see the impact of knee-jerk reaction rather than critical thinking to these safeguarding alerts.

THE OVERARCHING OBSERVATION

We are mindful that, throughout this book, and drawing upon observations from the training sessions, we might be seen as being critical of professionals and see them as the problem in online safeguarding. While reporting on observations, it is important to do so objectively without prejudice. It is clear from our discussions with young people that many do not trust adults who care for them when it comes to resolving issues related to online harms, and we cannot report on this.

However, we should stress that, in the majority of cases, professionals we have worked with on this project, and more widely in our practice, come from a well-intentioned place and want to do their best to support young people they work with. However, without effective support and training, their knowledge falls back upon what they have developed from their own social lives, the use of digital technology themselves, what they discuss with peers, and what they learn from the media. This is coupled with increasingly demands from regulators and government bodies to become compliant with ever changing guidance and poorly understood legal contexts. During the Headstart project, there have been three iterations of Keeping Children Safe in Education, changes in the inspection process around online safety, reams of non-statutory guidance, signposting to numerous resources and changes in curriculum, all of which the professionals are expected to respond to with little national guidance. As we have stated in Chapter 2—while the statutory demands make it clear professionals should be training in online safeguarding, deliver education in online safeguarding and have technical measures in place to ensure children and young people are "safe from online harm", there is little guidance on what good online safeguarding training and education looks like, just that they have to do it.

As we have observed above about gaining profession feedback prior to launch, we have also not had any new behaviours raised in training sessions. When asked for observations about the tool, professionals tended to be focussed upon specific technologies, and in some cases asked for lists of apps to be concerned about (we will discuss this in more detail below), or ways that can advise parents/carers to track and monitor young people's devices. We should bear in mind that these discussions took place after the professionals had done the pre-sessional online materials, in which there is a great deal of messaging about how we need to refocus from technology to behaviours and support.

Many professionals admit that they don't really know what young people do online, and have a minimal understanding of things like how privacy settings actually are and how they work. By way of example, in discussing YouTube in one training session, none of the professionals knew what sorts of videos young people watch on YouTube, that videos could be listed as "Unlisted" or what that meant, or that you could turn off comments (let alone how to). Yet figures show that 80% of people between 15 and 25 use YouTube (Statista 2021b), and it had the highest reach to this age group of *any* social media site in 2020 (Statista 2021a).

Professionals feel like they have to have all of the answers, to be the digital white knight and protect children in their care from the harms from being online, because they are told this is their statutory duty. However, this is not what we hear from young people—they do not want all of the answers, they want to get help and support. Even something when a professional, in response to a young person disclosing harm, evolves their response from "how could you have done that, how could you be so stupid?" to "ok, this happens, lets see what we can do about it", is progress. This does not require the professional to be in possession of a list of "top ten online harms this month" or to be on top of the latest case law related to children and illegal data collection. It just requires the confidence to realise this is not about technology, it is about supporting the child, and there are networks across the stakeholder space that can provide answers even if the professional does not have them immediately to hand.

One thing we have noticed in our discussions with professionals is moving the discourse from a preventative one to one of harm reduction that is generally viewed as positive and relatable. A lot of professionals were more comfortable with this approach, but had never considered it for online safeguarding. While harm reduction is well established in public health challenges (e.g. see Inciardi & Harrison, 1999), there is little work that considers online safeguarding from a harm reduction perspective.

By way of example, in one training session, where we had discussed a length the need to move away from the technology and look at the behaviour, and just because something is described on a platform the professional does not recognise does not mean they cannot help the young person, one attendee said "but what should I do when they say they buy drugs on snapchat?". We have touched on this topic before, in Chapter 3. Their view was this is problematic because, firstly, they do not know what SnapChat is and, secondly, surely this is worse because it is online. However, when we unpacked it from a perspective where they had received harm reduction training ("lets ignore the technology for the minute, what advice would you give to a young person saying they'd purchased some MDMA from someone in a pub carpark?") they could see that the advice could be the same, and it was about supporting the young person, rather than panicking about what SnapChat was.

We are often told by professionals that they have tried to talk to young people about online issues, and "they don't want to talk about them". This seems entire in conflict with our own experiences with young people. Indeed, during a follow-up session with a college we are working with, we conducted a focus group with some of their students very recently. The college has been using the tool for a year and feel they want to push through a "culture change" across the institution that is youth centric and develops confidence to disclose online harms. One aspect of this they wished to explore was a conversation with some students to understand what would work around discussing online safeguarding in their tutor sessions. One thing that came out very strongly from the students we talked with was that "discussion and questions" are far more useful than "PowerPoints and videos". They also made a very telling point that while they did not expect the tutor to have all of the answers, they did expect them to be able to manage the discussion to make sure everyone had chance to talk and it wasn't taken over by the loudest voices.

Throughout all of the focus groups with young people on this project, as well as our own wider practice, we find young people very willing to talk about their online lives. When we've asked, they've been more than happy to explain the intricacies of the apps, games and websites they spend their time on, as well as a willingness to share the practices they have to manage the risks they face.

Professionals perceive high levels of risk to young people online and want to do all they can to keep them safe. However, their perceptions are often flawed by a lack of understanding of what young people are doing online, and a lack of willingness on their part to explore this with each individual young person. They are looking for a one-size-fits-all approach that simply does not exist. We are also mindful that a lot of professionals ask for "the" resource, that will make all of these problems go away. Again, a preventative mindset, and a need to be the white knight, results in them needing "something" to stop all of this. This is in contrast to the needs expressed by young people, as raised by the discussion above, they do not want all of the answers, because there are few clear answers, they want help.

REFERENCES

Federal Trade Commission. (1998). *Children's Online Privacy Protection Act 1998.* https://www.ftc.gov/enforcement/rules/rulemaking-regulatory-reform-proceedings/childrens-online-privacy-protection-rule. Accessed August 2021.

Inciardi, J. A., & Harrison, L. D. (Eds.). (1999). *Harm reduction: National and international perspectives.* Sage.

Phippen, A., & Bond, E. (2019). *Digital ghost stories; impact, risks and reasons.* SWGfL. https://swgfl.org.uk/assets/documents/digital-ghost-stories-impact-risks-and-reasons-1.pdf. Accessed August 2021.

Robinson, G., McLean, R., & Densley, J. (2019). Working county lines: Child criminal exploitation and illicit drug dealing in Glasgow and Merseyside. *International Journal of Offender Therapy and Comparative Criminology, 63*(5), 694–711.

Statista. (2021a). *Reach of social media used by UK teens and young adults 2020 Published by H. Tankovska, Jan 25, 2021 The most-used social media site among teenagers and young adults in the United Kingdom (UK) in 2020 was YouTube. A survey carried out by AudienceProject r.* Statista. https://www.statista.com/statistics/1059462/social-media-usage-uk-age/. Accessed August 2021.

Statista. (2021b). *YouTube: share of social network website visits in the United Kingdom (UK) 2015–2021 Published by H. Tankovska, Apr 8, 2021 As of January 2021, YouTube held a market share of 2.46 percent among online social networking platforms in the United Kingdom (UK).* Statista. https://www.statista.com/statistics/280314/youtubes-social-network-market-share-in-the-united-kingdom-uk/. Accessed August 2021.

The European Union. (2016). *General Data Protection Regulation.* https://gdpr-info.eu/. Accessed August 2021.

UK Government. (2018). *Data Protection Act 2018.* https://www.legislation.gov.uk/ukpga/2018/12/contents/enacted. Accessed August 2021.

CHAPTER 7

Moving the Conversation On

Abstract The findings of the Headstart Kernow project have illustrated that there is still a gulf between the intentions of adults with safeguarding responsibilities and their good intentions, and the impact of these upon the young people they wish to support. A key finding in the project is the lack of formal training among professionals and how the resultant knowledge gaps are filled with digital value bias, drawn mainly from professional's own use of digital technology and opinions drawn from media reporting and peers. The COVID-19 pandemic, and subsequent lockdowns, has further illustrated that with a lack of evidence conjecture becomes fact and reinforces the findings of the Headstart Kernow research further.

Keywords COVID-19 · Digital value bias · Digital white knight · Everyone's Invited · Critical thinking

In conclusion, we draw this book to a close with a reflection of the findings of the Headstart project against the policy direction explored at the start and show that these findings do little to support such a prohibitive approach. We have seen, throughout the discussions in this book, a need from those we, as stakeholders in online safeguarding, wish to protect, that the "traditional" approaches to online safety are not working, and

A. Phippen and L. Street, *Online Resilience and Wellbeing in Young People*, Palgrave Studies in Cyberpsychology,
https://doi.org/10.1007/978-3-030-88634-9_7

rather than having a population of young people confident that they can disclose to any stakeholder and gain support, there are many who would rather try to sort thing out themselves, or suffer in silence, for fear that disclosure will result in chastisement or making matters worse. Young people certainly believe that there is a relationship between digital technology and their wellbeing but, equally, they do not believe the elimination of online harms is an achievable goal.

In drawing our discussions to a close, we will reflect upon two recent issues related to online safeguarding that further illustrate the points we are making, before considering the role of all stakeholders in online safeguarding, and what professionals can do to more effectively support young people in their care.

COVID-19 and Lockdown

Obviously, over the last two years, we have been experiencing young people engaging with their education online, and being subject to COVID-19-related lockdowns. While the broader safeguarding issues around this are beyond the scope of this book, there is one recurring issue that is very much related to our discussions. In April 2020, the NSPCC published an article NSPCC (2020) on their website stating:

> Lonely children are twice as likely to be groomed online.

And within the article there was a:

> Heightened risk of sexual abuse during coronavirus lockdown... The NCA knows from online chats that offenders are discussing opportunities to abuse children during the crisis and Europol has seen a surge in attempts by offenders to contact young people on social media.

What followed was a range of online safeguarding organisations and law enforcement agencies all coming out with similar messages. For example, the Internet Watch Foundation (IWF, 2020) raised concerns that:

> There are warnings that, with schools being forced to shut, there is an **increased risk** of children being groomed and coerced online.

The National Crime Agency (NCA, 2020) raised concerns that:

But the NCA also knows from online chat that offenders are **discussing opportunities** to abuse children during the Covid 19 crisis.

Interpol followed with a similar report (Interpol, 2020) which stated:

Boredom **may** lead to increased risk-taking, including an increase in the taking and sharing of self-generated material.

And even UNICEF put out an alert (UNICEF, 2020)

In South Africa, the current lockdown **may** put children's privacy in danger as they spend more time online.

Clearly, if one applies a knee-jerk reaction to lockdowns, it makes sense. Young people are locked down and online more; therefore, they are more at risk of grooming and abuse. However, it became apparent that when these reports were investigated in more detail, there was little evidence to support the claims, just suggested, as highlighted above, that it might be the case. For example, the Interpol report provided evidence that there was greater activity in the exchange of child abuse imagery during lockdowns, including the availability of self-produced material. However, it provided no evidence of increased reporting of grooming by young people or their families.

As we discussed in Chapter 6, these sort of safeguarding alerts tend to trigger reactions across the safeguarding profession, and these claims quickly became established as fact. We were told that children were more at risk during lockdown, and parents needed to monitor online access to ensure they were safe. However, when we explore that data on this, there is little evidence this was actually the case. In work still ongoing, we served a Freedom of Information request on all local authorities asking for a week on week breakdown of safeguarding disclosures received, with a separate breakdown for online abuse if possible. While the work is ongoing, we publish a brief report on initial findings in Phippen and Bada (2020). Furthermore, almost all local authorities replied to state they have no statutory requirement to categorise online abuse separately, and therefore, they do not, which begs the question—where is the evidence for this conjecture? We acknowledge that the Child Exploitation and

Online Protection Command (CEOP[1]), as the national organisation to report online abuse, might have experienced an increase and, as they are not subject to Freedom of Information, this is different to determine. However, they have not reported an increase in disclosures, and the NCA reporting stated:

> Since schools closed because of coronavirus the number of child safety concerns reported through the CEOP website has stayed largely the same.

Discussions with teaching staff with whom we have a relationship as a result of the Headstart Kernow work further confirm this—they have not experienced an increase in safeguarding disclosures as a result of lockdowns. While there has been a change in the nature of disclosures, the most serious that have been dealt with related to intra-familial domestic abuse. There has certainly not, in their view, been an increase in online harms as a result of these lockdowns. As one young person pointed out when we asked them about it, they are spending up to eight hours a day online for college work, they need a break from it after that and they are unlikely to then spend the evening, in their words "chatting to pedos".

This is certainly a clear example of the need for evidence to make informed and responsible alerts. Saying "children *may* be at increased risk" does little but create moral panic.

EVERYONE'S INVITED

The other recent phenomenon worthy of comment is the emergence of the Everyone's Invited website[2] and subsequent policy response, which both provides further evidence of the unwillingness of young people to disclose abuse and the failure of some very senior professionals to be informed by evidence.

The website, established by a victim of sexual abuse in their school, provides the means for survivors of abuse, who have been subjected to abuse by peers, to anonymously disclose what happened to them. These testimonies are then posted on the website. Since its establishment in June 2020, the website now hosts over 51,000 testimonials (at the time

[1] https://www.ceop.police.uk/. Accessed August 2021.

[2] https://www.everyonesinvited.uk/. Accessed August 2021.

of writing, that is certainly going to increase by the time of publication). The testimonies detail a breadth of abuse by peers, including a great deal of image based and online abuse. An examination of the testimonies shows, once again, that many survivors felt there was no point in disclosing because they would not be taken seriously, they believed/had been told what they had done was illegal, or, in the case of many who did disclose, they were told to not tell tales or simply "ignore" the abuse.

It is an evidence base that provides a great deal of validation to the data collected in this project. However, it is also the impact of the website on national policy that again illustrates the response by professionals. As a result of the volume of disclosures, and the nature of these, the Secretary of State for Education, Gavin Williamson, tasked the regulator, OFSTED, with an investigation of schools and colleges to determine prevalence of abuse. The report by OFSTED (2021) made it very clear this is extremely common, and in all of the schools they visited (32 in total), there were young people who disclosed abuse. The subsequent reporting in BBC News (Wills & Sellgren, 2021) reported on the "shocked" by those at a national policy level:

> Ofsted chief inspector Amanda Spielman said she was "shocked" that young people said it was a significant problem at every school the watchdog visited.

And Gavin Williamson said Ofsted's review had "rightly highlighted where we can take specific and urgent action to address sexual abuse in education".

Our concern is the level of shock by those who form national policy related to these issues. Speaking for ourselves, and having discussed with others, both academic and professional, there is no one who actually speaks regularly to young people who is "shocked" or surprised by the findings. We are further alarmed because the literature has existed for a long period of time to report on these sorts of abuses in school settings. Ringrose et al. (2012) produced an excellent qualitative study almost ten years ago that highlighted these issues. Furthermore, the House of Commons Women and Equalities Committee conducted an inquiry into these issues in 2016, and many of us provided evidence for this. The published report (Women & Equalities Committee, 2016) made it very clear that the evidence showed this was prevalent in schools and made a number of recommendations that, while falling on deaf ears at the time, are very similar to those suggested by OFSTED in their 2021 report. Put simply, anyone working in this area should not be shocked by the findings of the 2021 study because the evidence base has shown this for a long time. It is their lack of knowledge about the evidence base that is shocking.

The Ecology of Childhood
and Online Safeguarding

Returning the Bronfenbrenner's ecology of child development, as discussed in Chapter 2, we have shown throughout this book that it is the failures of stakeholders that result in poor outcomes for young people disclosing (or not disclosing) online abuse. As we have discussed above, the focus for most online safeguarding policy is prevention, generally through technical intervention by a single stakeholder (technology providers). With other stakeholders, assuming "someone else" is dealing with the issue; rather than focussing on their own professional development, we end up with a prohibitive discourse that is failing young people.

Research by Bond and Phippen (2019) developed the Bronfenbrenner ecology to the online world. By adapting this ecosystem for online safeguarding, it provides an illustration of the importance of stakeholder interaction and the breadth of stakeholder responsibilities for online safeguarding (Fig. 7.1).

The value of the model is that it shows many different stakeholders in online safeguarding and shows the importance of interactions (mesosystems) between them, as well as the distance a given stakeholder is from the child we wish to safeguard. It allows us to clearly see that this is not something that can be tackled by digital platforms, or a teacher at a school, without input from other stakeholders with safeguarding responsibilities.

From the broad online safeguarding, we need to ensure we do not lose focus on the roles in the microsystem, or the fact that encompassing all of this—the macrosystem—should be the rights of the child.

Within this model, the importance of rights is defined, with the UN Convention on the Rights of the Child as the fundamental macrosystem around while the entire stakeholder space in enveloped. While this should be any safeguarding professional's go-to for the development of new resources, teaching, technologies, policy or legislation, this seems to be the most neglected, and often ignore, aspect of online child safeguarding.

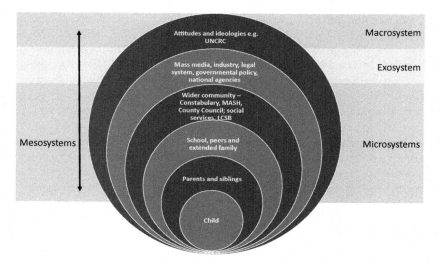

Fig. 7.1 A stakeholder model for child online safety

Arguably, it is sometimes viewed as a barrier for solutions, rather than the foundation of any legislative or policy development.

The findings of the Headstart Kernow digital resilience workpackage highlights the important of an integrated stakeholder approach to online safeguarding. The evidence from the project strongly supports the need for critical thinking by adults, supported with resource, so that they can help young people navigate the online world, rather than thinking they have all of the answers or need to stop them doing anything dangerous. Returning to the fundamental issues discussed with young people, as well as not being effective, prohibitive approaches create barriers between young people and those with caring responsibilities.

Young people need to be able to take risks online, in order to build resilience. But those risks need to be mitigated with support, and the knowledge that they can speak to adults about concerns they have, rather than shutting down for fear of being told off. Young people have told us throughout the project that they want to have conversations, they want to ask questions, and they would like those questions to be answered. However, they do not expect professionals to know it all, and "ill find that out for you" is a reasonable response in their view.

One of the most encouraging things to come out of the project is that there are a number of schools and colleges that are *confident in their lack of knowledge* to contact us should a safeguarding alert arise or a student discloses something they do not recognise. This is a significant step forward and reflects the importance of communication between stakeholders within the ecological model. The mesosystems are a crucial part of online safeguarding, there is no one stakeholder that can resolve every disclosure or, regardless of legislative intention, prevent all online harms. And while we are often able to help schools and colleges who are reaching out, equally if we do not have the answer, we can use our own networks to resolve issues. Working together is far more effective that trying to solve everything oneself for fear of admission that perhaps one does not have all of the answers.

In conclusion, we would make the following recommendations for all professionals working with children and young people:

When it comes to online safeguarding, prohibition is not the solution. You cannot make a child safe online; however, you can help them build resilience and understand the risks faced going online.

Work at your digital value bias. We all bring our own experiences to our professional work environment, whether this is through personal experiences, or as a parent. It is important to be mindful of these, and to challenge them when making safeguarding judgements. While we might believe a young person has been irresponsible in taking an intimate image and sending it to a partner, the fact is, from a safeguarding scenario the only thing upon which to focus is "how can I help this young person who has disclose upset or harm". Telling them that you do not believe they should have do something in the first place will not help.

Don't be a digital white knight. A professional does not have to have all of the answers, or protect every young person in their care from the potential for any harm online. Just as young people experience harm and abuse offline, they will also experience it online. We can work with them to recognise the risks and mitigate them. And, if they do experience harm, they need to be confident they can disclose and get support.

Most importantly, professionals need to understand that they do not have to have all of the answers, and the most crucial part of the safeguarding response is to listen to young people. We have shown throughout the project that young people want to talk about their own lives, and they have many questions. "Don't do it" is not an answer they want to hear.

REFERENCES

Bond, E., & Phippen, A. (2019). Why is placing the child at the centre of online safeguarding so difficult? *Entertainment Law Review, 30*(3), 80–84.

Internet Watch Foundation. (2020). *Children may be at greater risk of grooming during coronavirus pandemic as IWF braces for spike in public reports.* https://www.iwf.org.uk/news/children-may-be-at-greater-risk-of-grooming-during-coronavirus-pandemic-as-iwf-braces-for. Accessed August 2021.

Interpol. (2020). *Threats and trends in child sexual exploitation and abuse— COVID-19 impact.* https://www.interpol.int/en/content/download/ 15611/file/COVID19%20-%20Child%20Sexual%20Exploitation%20and% 20Abuse%20threats%20and%20trends.pdf. Accessed August 2021.

National Crime Agency. (2020). *Law enforcement in coronavirus online safety push as National Crime Agency reveals 300,000 in UK pose sexual threat to children.* https://www.nationalcrimeagency.gov.uk/news/onlinesaf etyathome. Accessed August 2021.

NSPCC. (2020). *Lonely children are twice as likely to be groomed online.* NSPCC. https://www.nspcc.org.uk/about-us/news-opinion/2020/ coronavirus-children-groomed-online. Accessed August 2020.

OFSTED. (2021). *Review of sexual abuse in schools and colleges.* https://www. gov.uk/government/publications/review-of-sexual-abuse-in-schools-and-colleges/review-of-sexual-abuse-in-schools-and-colleges#what-did-we-find-out-about-the-scale-and-nature-of-sexual-abuse-in-schools. Accessed August 2021.

Phippen, A., & Bada, M. (2020). *COVID lockdowns and online harms.* https:// www.cambridgecybercrime.uk/COVID/COVIDbriefing-13.pdf. Accessed August 2021.

Ringrose, J., Gill, R., Livingstone, S., & Harvey, L. (2012). *A qualitative study of children, young people and 'sexting': A report prepared for the NSPCC.* NSPCC. https://letterfromsanta.nspcc.org.uk/globalassets/documents/res earch-reports/qualitative-study-children-young-people-sexting-report.pdf. Accessed August 2021.

UNICEF. (2020). *Children at increased risk of harm online during global COVID-19 pandemic.* UNICEF. https://www.unicef.org/southafrica/press-releases/children-increased-risk-harm-online-during-global-covid-19-pan demic-unicef. Accessed August 2021.

Wills, E., & Sellgren, K. (2021). *Girls asked for nudes by up to 11 boys a night, Ofsted finds.* BBC News. https://www.bbc.co.uk/news/education-574 11363. Accessed August 2021.

Women and Equalities Committee. (2016). *Sexual harassment and sexual violence in schools.* https://publications.parliament.uk/pa/cm201617/cmselect/cmw omeq/91/9102.htm. Accessed August 2021.

Appendix: Online Resilience Tool

Note The most up to date version of the Online Resilience Tool can be found at: https://www.headstartkernow.org.uk/digital-resilience/.

What is digital resilience? Digital resilience is a dynamic personality asset that grows from digital activation, i.e. through engaging with appropriate opportunities and challenges online, rather than through avoidance and safety behaviours (UK Council for Internet Safety, Digital Resilience Framework, September 2019).

Using the Tool

The Online Resilience Tool is a practical way to assess young people's online behaviour and help you make a decision about whether that behaviour represents risk of harm.

Behaviours are organised by age group and divided into "Not harmful", "Potentially harmful" and "Harmful". The majority of behaviours young people engage in online will fall into the "Not harmful" section. There is no way of completely eradicating risk in the online world, in the same way as we cannot completely eradicate it in the offline world; however, we can reduce risk through interventions and support which will be discussed at the end of this document.

When using the tool you should always consider the wider context of the young person's life. If the young person is less mature, you may want to assess their behaviour based on a lower age group. Equally, if you know certain behaviours are unsafe for a young person, you should use that information to make a safeguarding decision; for example, if a young person has severe body image issues and starts posting a large number of selfies, this could be an indicator of a problem.

Below are explanations of the "Not harmful", "Potentially harmful" and "Harmful" categories, followed by the tool and information on how to respond to identified behaviour.

Not Harmful

These behaviours are normal and can be considered low risk for the young person and people around them. The young person interacts with the online world in a variety of ways, while also having a range of interests and activities outside of it, including interacting with their peers offline. The young person enjoys the activities they engage in online. As they grow older, they will be more private about their online activities, and they may increasingly use technology to organise their social lives. Young people may interact with adults through appropriate forums, such as online games, but will mainly interact with peers.

For older teenagers, some behaviours in this category may conflict with parents' or professionals' values but reflect normal adult behaviours.

Note Once a behaviour is in the 'Not harmful' column it will remain in that column for every subsequent age group.

Potentially Harmful

These behaviours may indicate a risk of harm to the young person or someone else.

Potentially harmful behaviours mean you must have a conversation with the young person (or their parent/carer depending on their age) to find out more. Potentially harmful behaviours **only** show that more information is needed to assess the risk of harm, or actual harm to the young person. Once more information is received you should be able to identify whether the behaviour is harmful or not.

Harmful

These behaviours represent a high risk of harm to the young person or other young people. The young person may be doing them compulsively and may experience withdrawal symptoms if the behaviour is stopped or curtailed. They may be a victim of intimidating or humiliating treatment online or may be the perpetrator of this, which could include bribery, trickery or threat of violence. The young person is likely to be highly secretive about their online activities, beyond what might be considered a normal desire for privacy.

These behaviours may be inappropriate for the young person's age. This may be through the young person spending a lot of time interacting with older people, or engaging in activities beyond their developmental stage.

Any behaviour that involves accessing illegal content is a harmful behaviour.

If you identify a Harmful behaviour, you will need to act immediately and offer follow-up support (see below for suggestions on this).

Note If you see a behaviour in Harmful, it would also be Harmful for all younger age groups.

NB: You will not see the term cyberbullying throughout the Online Resilience Traffic Light Tool. We have left it out because any of the behaviours may indicate that bullying is taking place and cyberbullying is not distinct from offline bullying.

Age	Not harmful	Potentially harmful	Harmful
0–5 y/o	Playing age-appropriate games with a family member (aimed at this age group, consider PEGI rating) Role modelling age-appropriate characters Being aware of/being told there is "adult content" online Asking to have a photo removed/not put on social media Watching films/TV with family member Supervised Skyping with remote family members Interacting with a digital device Watching age-appropriate digital content with friends Interest/involvement in family social media, e.g. looking at news feed, asking to see pictures Curiosity around digital devices A variety of interactions and responses to devices Being left alone with a device with parental controls in place for up to 10 minutes Talking about how they feel if they see something upsetting	Gaming alone Preoccupation with digital devices Reaching for a device as soon as they wake up Using screens less than an hour before bedtime	Watching a family member play age-restricted games Role-playing or parroting adult content (e.g. sex/violence) Watching adult content Being left with a tablet/smartphone unsupervised for 30 minutes or more Upset or aggressive response to withdrawal of device (beyond what is normal for the child) Sexual or violent language Having their own social media account Use of digital devices after bedtime

Age	Not harmful	Potentially harmful	Harmful
6–8 y/o	Age-appropriate gaming with adult supervision Filming themselves/friends playing age-appropriate games Guided research/learning Supervised schoolwork using online technology Messaging friends on shared devices Watching online content on a device with parental controls Taking but not sending selfies Playing with filters Sharing images with peers with parent/guardian oversight	Being left with a tablet/smartphone unsupervised for 30 minutes or more Gaming alone Gaming with fantasy violence (e.g. cartoons) Multi-player online gaming Secretive use of online device Ownership of their own devices Accidental access of sexual content Mimicking online behaviour Being obsessed with selfies Posing all the time Being obsessed with celebrities, wanting to be a celebrity Ganging up on or isolating others online Accidentally sending selfies Knowing passwords to parental devices Having their own social media account Sharing passwords	Use of digital devices after bedtime Contact with strangers online Sexual or violent language Accessing pornography Sexualised posing Requesting images to be airbrushed Sharing indecent or distressing images with peers

Age	Not harmful	Potentially harmful	Harmful
9–12 y/o	Gaming (on or offline) in line with age restrictions Doing homework alone Learning how devices work with supervision Learning how to write code with supervision Looking at social media with friends/family Sending friends direct messages Group messaging with friends Sharing things seen online with friends in person Making content and publishing online Having a private social media account Having private direct messages Posing all the time Using filters on pictures Meeting online friends with a parent or carer present	Playing age-restricted games Receiving gifts in online games from family members Watching films/TV online alone Using of digital platforms without parents/guardians knowledge Regular social media use Online interaction with strangers Having a YouTube channel/actively promoting it among peers Talking about high numbers of subscribers/followers on online cast/social media channels (for example YouTube/Instagram) Being obsessed with celebrities, wanting to be a celebrity Accessing pornography as a one off Becoming an influencer/brand ambassador Excessively sharing personal information online Sharing social media/device passwords with others Taking selfies all the time Ganging up on or isolating others online Having a public social media account	Disrupted sleep through device dependence/gaming Receiving gifts in online games from strangers (someone unknown to parents) Use of digital devices after bedtime Online gambling Researching issues in an unsupported way, e.g. self-harm/depression, eating disorders Searching for information on losing weight Using fake social media accounts to trick or humiliate others Sexualised posing online Sending/receiving nudes/Sexting Frequent access to pornography Requesting images to be airbrushed Placing oneself at physical risk in order to take selfies or generate online content Anxiety around digital communications Being secretive* about direct messages Accessing extremist websites Repeating extremist views read about online Accessing illegal content Online dating Meeting online friends unsupervised

Age	Not harmful	Potentially harmful	Harmful
13–15 y/o	Learning how devices work Learning how to write software Using reliable sources to find out about personal issues (Brook, Talk to Frank, NHS direct) Posting content on social media Instagram/Snapchat stories One to one messaging Group messaging and opting to leave or mute a group chat Commenting on a status Accidentally receiving nudes Having a YouTube channel Running Snapchat streaks with friends Blocking and reporting someone for posting inappropriate content Asking to have a photo removed/not put on social media Removing a picture of someone else when asked Having celebrity role models, aspiring to be like a celebrity Private use of digital platforms Meeting online friends supervised	Playing older age-restricted games with parental consent Searching for information on losing weight Writing a blog Use of digital devices after bedtime Preoccupation with selfies Excessive posing Requesting images to be airbrushed Sharing social media/device passwords with others Being secretive* about direct messages Ganging up on or isolating others online Fear of missing out leading to separation anxiety from social media Setting up a fake social media account to explore gender identity or sexuality Regular use of pornography Online dating with peers Sending/receiving nudes/Sexting Accessing deep web*** sites using browsers such as Tor to explore what is there	Disrupted sleep through device dependence/gaming Online gambling Using unreliable sites to find out about personal issues Accessing pro-self-harm or pro-ana (pro-anorexia) sites Passive social media use, i.e. just scrolling, never commenting or messaging Setting up a fake social media account/pretending to be someone else online to trick or humiliate others Placing oneself at physical risk in order to take selfies or generate online content Compulsive** use of social media including checking during the night Refusing to remove a picture of someone else when asked Coercive behaviour towards others using digital technology (for example tracking others, accessing other people's accounts) Compulsive** use of pornography Watching violent/extreme pornography Sexual webcamming Pressuring someone to send nudes/sext

(continued)

(continued)

Age	Not harmful	Potentially harmful	Harmful
			Accessing extremist websites
			Repeating extremist views read about online
			Accessing dark web*** to engage with services (for example buying drugs online, downloading extreme pornography)
			Accessing illegal content
			Showing someone distressing videos they don't want to see
			Online dating with adults
			Forwarding nudes of other young people, including to friends, without consent

Age	Not harmful	Potentially harmful	Harmful
16–18 y/o	Writing a blog Research for school/college Looking at images of different body types/genital types to understand range of normal Finding out about sexual behaviours using pornography Private use of digital platforms Setting up a fake social media account to explore gender identity or sexuality Online dating with peers (while taking appropriate precautions such as taking a friend and meeting in public) Meeting online friends if have skyped/facetimed (while taking appropriate precautions) Online shopping with own money	Online gambling Use of digital devices after bedtime Obsession with selfies Excessive posing in selfies Requesting images to be airbrushed Catfishing/direct messaging someone pretending to be someone else Excessively watching porn Being secretive* about direct messages Meeting online friends unsupervised Meeting online friends as part of a group Taking and sending/receiving nudes/sexting for any reason Online dating with adults Accessing deep web*** sites using browsers such as Tor to explore what is there	Disrupted sleep through device dependence/gaming Accessing pro-self-harm/suicide sites Accessing extremist/pro-self-harm/suicide social media accounts as part of ongoing recovery or offering support Placing oneself at physical risk in order to take selfies or generate online content Coercive behaviour towards others using digital technology (for example tracking others, accessing other people's accounts) Retention of indecent images of peers Sexual webcamming Selling nudes Compulsive** use of pornography Accessing extreme pornography Radicalisation (this could be through specific extremist sites or through seemingly innocent forums such as those attached to games) Accessing extremist websites Forwarding nudes of other young people, including to friends, without consent Persistently viewing extremist sites Repeating extremist views read about online Accessing dark web*** to engage with services (for example buying drugs online, downloading extreme pornography) Accessing illegal content Showing someone distressing videos they don't want to see Online shopping with parents/carers' money without their knowledge

(continued)

*Secretive—young people have a right to privacy, and as such may not want to show a parent or carer messages sent to peers. However, sometimes this may go beyond a normal expectation of privacy; for example, if a young person becomes very agitated about someone seeing their messages, it could be a sign that they are being bullied, groomed or exploited online

**Compulsive—this is behaviour that is getting in the way of the young person doing what might normally be expected of them, for example if they stop seeing friends, completing school work, etc. This differs from excessive behaviour which may still happen very frequently but not to the point it is interfering with normal activities. In having a conversation with a young person about excessive behaviour, it is important to determine whether this behaviour is actually compulsive or more of a habit

***Deep web/dark web—the deep web is any website that is not indexed by search engines such as google. Accessing these sites is untraceable and they are often used to circumvent tracking that may be put on young people's devices. The deep web is not inherently illegal; however, any young person using deep or dark web sites is incredibly vulnerable and therefore support should be offered even if they are accessing them for legitimate reasons (such as not wanting a parent to know they are exploring their gender or sexuality). The dark web refers to areas of the deep web where illegal activity takes place. Often, young people will use these terms interchangeably

What to Do When You Have Identified a Behaviour

Most of the online behaviour young people engage in will fall into the "Not Harmful" category. All of the online activities young people engage in can give you information about the young person's life, interests and concerns, which can in turn help you to engage with a young person, building a warm and understanding relationship. Expressing identity through online behaviour is a normal part of a young person's life. Professionals can sometimes feel intimidated by talk of apps and games that are unfamiliar and this can lead to being dismissive of activities that are important to a young person's identity, or overreacting to activities that are normal and low risk. This tool avoids naming specific apps or games* and instead encourages professionals to use their existing skills and knowledge to respond to behaviours. When a "Not Harmful" behaviour is identified, professionals can offer guidance and support to ensure healthy development continues. This could be through group or one-to-one sessions considering what risks people might face in the future and how they think those risks could be managed; for example, it would be appropriate to discuss risks of online dating with 14- to 16-year-olds and ask them how they might manage these risks.

Where behaviours are not age-appropriate, or represent harm to the young person or others, adults must intervene to help the young person and prevent further harm. We all have a duty to safeguard children and young people. You should refer to your organisation's safeguarding policy or report to the police or social services where appropriate. This tool aims to help you identify harmful behaviours, once identified you should use your safeguarding policy to proceed. We have listed some suggestions of how to respond to Harmful or Potentially Harmful behaviours below, but this does not replace or supersede your organisation's safeguarding procedures.

When planning how to respond to a Harmful or Potentially Harmful behaviour, consider what support you might need to put in place to help the young person. For example, if a young person is being abusive to other people online, they may need to have an intervention focussed on understanding the consequences of their behaviour, whereas if they have been sharing nude images of themselves they may need some self-esteem work, or their whole peer group may need some education on the risks and consequences of this behaviour.

Other ways to respond to Harmful or Potentially Harmful behaviours:

- Giving the child or young person information or signposting to reliable websites
- Giving families information and signposting or referring to services
- Modelling behaviour—such as social media accounts set to private, time away from screens, etc.
- Identifying safe adults they can go to when they have questions
- Discussing precautions and ways of managing risk both on and offline
- Having consistency between home, family, school, community settings
- Having consistently enforced expectations of behaviour
- Extracting them from situations where they are experiencing themselves or causing harm to others
- Limiting access to technology when behaviour becomes problematic (although cutting a young person off from technology completely may make them more vulnerable or force their behaviour underground)

*Some police forces release lists of apps and games of concern to professionals.

The Role of Education

The Online Resilience Tool will be an invaluable resource in the delivery of the Relationships Education, Relationships and Sex Education (RSE) and Health Education curriculum, as it helps professionals to manage and moderate discussions and lesson delivery around normal, unusual and abnormal online behaviours for a given age group. For the primary curriculum, a lot of the behaviours listed in the tool will be addressed within the "Online Relationships" part of the curriculum. However, it will also support potential issues arising from areas such as "Being Safe" and "Respectful Relationships" as well. For secondary education, the tool primarily maps on to the "Online and Media" part of the curriculum but also supports issues raised in areas such as "Respectful Relationships", "Being Safe" and "Intimate and Sexual Relationships".

More information on the RSE curriculum can be found at: https://www.gov.uk/government/publications/relationships-education-relationships-and-sex-education-rse-and-health-education.

Online Behaviour and the Law

There is much discussion around legal issues around online behaviour and they are generally unhelpful and can lead to problematic outcomes for young people we are aiming to help. This section intends to provide clarification on a number of these issues:

Minors accessing pornography: It is not illegal for a minor to access pornography (as long as the pornography is legal), and they should not be told they have broken the law if they disclose they have accessed it. However, it is illegal to show a minor pornography, so if they have disclosed they have seen it, there is value in exploring how they have been exposed to it.

Accessing social media: There is a common belief that it is illegal for children to access social media under the age of 13. This is based upon US legislation that says it is illegal to advertise to a minor under the age of 13 without parental consent. More recently, the Data Protection Act 2018 states that a minor under the age of 13 is not capable of consenting to their data being collected. However, neither of these legal issues mean if someone under the age of 13 has a social media account is breaking the law and they should not be told such. They are, however, breaching the terms and conditions of the social media site, as they have not been honest about their date of birth when they signed up. As such they are potentially at more risk because the social media site can claim no responsibility if they are subject to abuse. These are all reasons why we should be supporting minors who disclose upset arising from social media when they are under the age of 13.

Sexting/sharing nudes: It is illegal for a minor to take an indecent image of themselves and send it to someone else. The law is defined in the 1978 Protection of Children Act, a piece of legislation developed to protect children from exploitation in the production of pornography. It never envisaged a time where the taker and sharer of the indecent image of a minor is also the subject of the image. While young people have been charged under this act as a result of sharing nudes, in general it is the view of the Crown Prosecution Service that it is rarely in the public interest (unless there is coercive, abuse or repetitive behaviours) to prosecute a minor under this act. Since 2016, police have been able to record such a crime as an "outcome 21". This means the crime is acknowledged but there is no public interest in pursuing a criminal case. We should not simply tell young people that sending nudes is illegal, as we risk re-victimising those who are being abused as a result of taking and sending an image. We should support them and help them resolve the issue, and involve law enforcement for their protection, not criminalisation.

Upskirting: Upskirting (the taking of an image or video from beneath someone's skirt using a mobile device) has recently been made illegal, in order to prevent people from engaging in these practices and to protect those who have been subject to this. While the recent Keeping Children Safe in Education update has raised the use of this legislation in schools to deter this behaviour among peers. However, this legislation is untested in the criminalisation of minors. While these behaviours are problematic among young peers, and warrants discussion and investigation, we have concerns that threatening minors with criminalisation as a result of these behaviour is disproportionate and counter-productive.

Online Gambling: There is strict legislation around age limits for online gambling. The majority of online gambling has an age limit set at 18 and covers things like online betting systems, casinos, sports betting, etc. However, there are some forms of online gambling such as the national lottery and scratch cards (both of which can be carried out online) that have an age limit of 16. Other forms of "soft" gambling (such as loot boxes) are currently unregulated and are often in games played by younger children. While there is nothing inherently dangerous about loot boxes, professionals should be aware that there is a potentially compulsive element to purchasing them and people of all ages might spend excessive amounts of money on them.

GLOSSARY

Child Sex Abuse Images: indecent images of children, either sexualised or engaged in sexual abuse. Often incorrectly referred to as "Child Pornography".

Coercion: using threats or bribery to try to force someone to do something they would otherwise not want to do. Threats could be subtle, normalised within a relationship or group of friends, and with the coerced individual being told that other people would do/are doing it when that may not be the case (therefore differing from peer pressure). There will often be an element of fear, meaning that the coerced individual may concede in an attempt to get the coercion/contact to end.

Critical Thinking: being able to assess the validity of claims made through a variety of media. This could involve fact checking through websites such as Snopes, or using Google Scholar to see only peer reviewed academic articles. It is important not to assume everything read online is false however as this can lead to apathy.

Cyberbullying: online bullying, which is now frequently, and unfortunately, used to describe any kind of online abuse. Bullying requires some level of threat (either physical or emotional) and also requires persistent abuse. Its inaccurate use allows us to both overreact to what we might refer to as brief online fallouts, and devalue the impact of different types of abuse, for example harassment.

A. Phippen and L. Street, *Online Resilience and Wellbeing in Young People*, Palgrave Studies in Cyberpsychology, https://doi.org/10.1007/978-3-030-88634-9

Dark Web: specific parts of the deep web where illegal activity takes place. This may be the exchange of child sex abuse images, images of bestiality and illegal forms of pornography. It may also include the planning of criminal activity such as drug dealing or terrorism.

Deep Web: simply parts of the World Wide Web that are "hidden" from search engines and monitoring because all communication and access is encrypted and needs to be accessed using special software such as Tor browsers. While the dark web is used for criminal activities, the deep web is often used by those wishing to avoid government or state monitoring, particularly under totalitarian regimes.

Digital Age of Consent: the age in law where is has been decided a child is capable of giving consent to have their data collected online. As part of the GDPR, this age has been defined in the UK as 13. The digital age of consent is frequently used to argue why younger children should not be using online services and how it is illegal for them to do so. This is not the case, and the law has not been established for any safeguarding reasons. It is no coincidence that the Digital Age of Consent is the same as the age defined in the US's Children Online Privacy Protection Act (COPPA), the law that restricts social media companies based there to collect the data of children without parental consent.

Extreme Pornography: pornographic content defined as illegal in sections 63–67 of the Criminal Justice and Immigration Act 2008, for example bestiality or pornography depicting physical harm. While possession of most pornography is not illegal, the possession of extreme pornography is and can lead to a custodial sentence.

Influencer: someone on social media who makes recommendations for purchasing of products or services in exchange for payment. Influencers are generally individuals with large online followings (hence it being valuable they make recommendations) and generate considerable income, hence "becoming an influencer" is attractive to young people. However, in order to develop a large following the individual needs to potentially expose themselves to risky online behaviours.

Online Grooming: making use of digital technology, such as social media or private messaging to trick, force or pressure a young person into engaging in sexual activity, for example sending an indecent image or live webcamming. While it is usual to expect grooming to take place between an adult and a child, grooming can take place at a peer-to-peer level too.

Online Grooming Re-radicalisation and Gangs: young people may be groomed using many of the same techniques into gangs or radicalised thinking. This may go alongside face-to-face grooming, making it very difficult for the young person to have any thinking space or time away from the person who is grooming them.

Online Peer on Peer Abuse: peer-on-peer abuse is any form of physical, sexual, emotional and financial abuse, and coercive control, exercised between children and within children's relationships (both intimate and non-intimate). Online peer-on-peer abuse is any form of peer-on-peer abuse with a digital element, for example, sexting, online abuse, coercion and exploitation, peer-on-peer grooming, threatening language delivered via online means, distribution of sexualised content and harassment.

Online Radicalisation: someone being influenced to adopt an extreme or radical position on social or political issues using online means (messaging, persuasive media, etc.), for example to get someone to adopt a far-right or Islamism ideology.

Pornography: is defined in the digital economy act 2017 as any image, video, work classified as "R18"—a special and legally restricted classification primarily for explicit works of consenting sex or strong fetish material involving adults.

Revenge Porn: the non-consensual sharing of an indecent image or video with others. It is important to take the legal distinction that one can only be a victim of revenge pornography if one is an adult, because it is not illegal for someone aged 18 and above to be the subject of a sexually explicit image.

Screentime: the term usually used to refer to how much time someone has spent online. While there is much concern regarding how much time young people spend online, there is insufficient evidence to show any clear impacts on mental health. However, recent advice by the Chief Medical Officer (https://assets.publishing.service.gov.uk/government/uploads/system/uploads/attachment_data/file/777026/UK_CMO_commentary_on_screentime_and_social_media_map_of_reviews.pdf) suggests a cautionary approach and not to dismiss screentime as a factor that has no impact on young people's mental health.

Sexting: the popular term for the exchange of indecent images using online or mobile devices (and sometimes used to describe sexualised messages). While the exchange of images such as this among young people is illegal, the legislation is complex and simple messages like "don't do it, it's illegal" will isolate those who might be being coerced or abused as a result of engaging in these activities. Young people are unlikely to apply the term "sexting" to their behaviour, but may use terms such as "nudes", "dick pic", "tit pic", etc.

Sexually Explicit Image/Video: an image or video which shows an individual, couple or group of people in a sexual context. This could be naked or fully clothed, undertaking or simulating a sexual act, or being filmed or photographed unknowingly.

Sharenting: the excessive, and often non-consensual, sharing of images and videos of their child(ren) online by parents without sufficient consideration of the impact of this on the child.

Trolling: deliberately starting an argument or upsetting people online for one's own amusement. Saying something controversial online to upset others.

Webcamming: using a webcam to live broadcast an interaction/performance, often of a sexual nature, sometimes in exchange for money but also used in grooming.

INDEX

© The Editor(s) (if applicable) and The Author(s), under exclusive   123
license to Springer Nature Switzerland AG 2022
A. Phippen and L. Street, *Online Resilience and Wellbeing in Young
People*, Palgrave Studies in Cyberpsychology,
https://doi.org/10.1007/978-3-030-88634-9

Printed by Printforce, United Kingdom